CHESHIRE

Edited by Claire Tupholme

First published in Great Britain in 2003 by
YOUNG WRITERS
Remus House,
Coltsfoot Drive,
Peterborough, PE2 9JX
Telephone (01733) 890066

HB ISBN 1 84460 028 9
SB ISBN 1 84460 029 7

FOREWORD

Young Writers was established in 1991 as a foundation for promoting the reading and writing of poetry amongst children and young adults. Today it continues this quest and proceeds to nurture and guide the writing talents of today's youth.

From this year's competition Young Writers is proud to present a showcase of the best poetic talent from across the UK. Each hand-picked poem has been carefully chosen from over 66,000 'Hullabaloo!' entries to be published in this, our eleventh primary school series.

This year in particular we have been wholeheartedly impressed with the quality of entries received. The thought, effort, imagination and hard work put into each poem impressed us all and once again the task of editing was a difficult but enjoyable experience.

We hope you are as pleased as we are with the final selection and that you and your family will continue to be entertained with *Hullabaloo! Cheshire* for many years to come.

CONTENTS

Christchurch Primary School

Christopher Alliston	19
Hannah Trousdale	20
Daniel Carter	20
Andrew Arathoon	21
Rachel Davies	21
Philip Arathoon	22
Amanda Parker	22
Kathryn Stanley	23
Andrew Banks	23
Ryan Bedwell	23
Chloe Green	24
Steven Carr	24
Laura May Page	24
Sean Clare	25
Joshua Kavanagh	25
Daniel Hughes	25
Lauren Caldwell	26
Jonathon Revell	26
Jessica Birt	26
Chloe Bebbington	27

Gorse Hall Primary School

Becci Heath	27
Sophie Whittaker	28
Adrienne Taylor	28
Evan Galloway	29
Chloe Troy	29
Thomas Manson & Shaun Evans	30
Lorna Davenport	30
Rebecca Geraghty	31
Chelsey Careless	31
Hannah Griffin	32
Jack Westwell	32
Emily Ormrod	33
Taylor Yates	33
Daniel Love	34
Amy Miller	35

Hursthead Junior School

Carolyn Luo Ward	53
Hannah McBride	54
Josh Atkinson	54
Scott Cockerham	55
Alice Kaiser	55
Ellen Powell	56
Bethany Simpson	56
Jonathan Cresswell	57
Georgia Newman	57
Jessica Mostyn	58
Robert Hart	58
Sophie McCarthy	59
Melissa Matos	59
Hannah Simpson	60
Autumn Corry	60
Anna Carley	60
Luke Daniels	61
Sarah Daisy Kirkham	61
Alexander Read	62
Matt Richardson	62
Katherine King	62
Kate Buxton	63
Benjamin Ashton	63
Charlotte Gabbitas	64
Max Hartle	64
Hannah Farrell	64
Aidan Nahirny	65
Lewis Walls	65
Aimée Mounfield	65
Alexandra Stone	66
Thomas Bolton	66
Michael Graham	67
Melissa Wilkinson	68
Ella Bucknall	69
Rebekah Dean	70
Jack Worne	71
Jack Moores	72
Matthew Bailey	72

Samuel Bradley	73
Bethany Williams	73
Becky Dawson	74
Matthew Kirton	74
Verity Rushton	75
Ben Porter	76
Lauren Bowden	76
Adam Crowder	77
Emily Grencis	78
Olivia McGahey	79
Megan Worne	80
James Manton	81
Oliver Bristow	82
Matthew Wells	82
Alice Semple	83
Grace Hetherington	84
Christopher Browne	84
Nicola Macleod	85
Jonathan Coates	85
James Cresswell	86
Ryan Healy	87
Katie Thompson	88
Philip Hanson	88
Rebecca Thomas	89
Nick Delap	89
Daniel Newman	90
Sophie Fletcher	90
David Coates	91
Elizabeth Kelly	91
Charles Hartle	92
Francesca Miller	93
Sam Roe	94
Matthew Drury	94
William Haddington	95
Adam Ramsden-Smith	95
Gemma Kiersey	96
Alex Fripp	96
Michael Roe	97

Hannah Rakestraw	97
Jonathan Chappell	98
Kate Earnshaw	98
Amie Thompson	99
Ben Devereux	99
Elizabeth Henshall	100
Matthew Oates	101
Thomas Mortimer	102
Patrick Bucknall	102
Matthew Clarke	103
Colin Todd	103
Katie Eddleston	104
Jack Green	104
Robert Blease	105
Katie Dawson	105
Jade Galtry-Smith	106
Lydia Ross	106
Nyall Bhatt	107
Andrew Powell	107
Chloe Dowdle	108
Philip Kent	109

Kingsley CP School

Emma Potter	110
Hayley Wright	110
Lucy Philpot	111
Edward Cox	111
Anna Feldman	112
Cassie Hesketh	113
Hannah Francis	114
Joshua Roberts	114
Esme Curtis	115
Jessica Elliott	115
Dyfed Thomas	116
Sam Saunders	116
Hannah Pomfret	117
Holly Byrne	117
Bryan Wright	118

Offley Junior School

St John's CE Primary School, Sandbach Heath

Shocklach Primary School

Claire Hellingman	181
Oliver Delf-Rowlandson	181
Rebecca Thomas	182
Charlotte Jenkins	182
Ryan Michael Jones	183
William Davies	183
Fraser Clark	184
Emma Ewins	185
Sam Westrip	185
Daryl Baker	186
Helen Duley	186
Aisling Cooter	186
Tabitha Lord	187
Alice Charlton	187
Sarah Hellingman	188

The Firs School

Alice Walton	188
Kitty Green	189
Katie Greenwood	189
Roseanna Yeoward	190
Camilla Bird	190
Lucy Smalley	191
Becky Okell	191
Catharine Verity	192

Wincham CP School

Nathan Turnbull & Dominic Percival	192
Scott Liddle & Connor Mills	192
Olivia Gillespie & Rebecca Paton	193
David Short	193
Bianca Huyton	194
Thomas Speak	194
Rhys Burton	195
Megan Rourke	195
Jake Smith & Michael Blythe	196
Oliver Pemble	196

Rebekka Millington & Carys Williams	196
Rachel Pogson	197
Samantha Payne & Stephanie Berry	197
Sophie Snelson & Mel Hughes	198
Cara Evans	198
Michael Evans	198
Tom Baker	199
Adam Nield	199
Sophie Massey	199
Cameron Fairweather	200
Benjamin James	200
Sam Apperley	200
Nic Clawson	201

Winnington Park Primary School

Carey Griffiths	201
Tom Mills	202
Tom Fishwick	202
Jack Slater	203
Aysha Barrett	203
Robyn Conway	204
Emma Brown	204
Annabel Johnson	204
Becky Healey	205
Lauren Edwards	205
Omar Smith	206
Hannah Gregory	206
Ashleigh Fullwood	206
Chloe Johnson	207
Kirsty Hassall	207
Tommy Bullen	208
Daniel Hayes	208
Rachel Bousfield	209
Sher Tang	209

Woodfield Primary School

Adam Woods	209
Chloe Hunt	210

The Poems

My Sister Put Me On The Transfer List

On offer:
One great skater, nine years old
He's better than anybody I know
He's quite a show-off when he does it
Guaranteed to fall over once or twice
This is a free transfer
But, he comes with a great many worries
He comes in from skating covered in bruises
Then he ignores you and slams the doors
He's always eating rubbish
He never eats his veg
He's OK at school
But homework's not his thing
He's always answering people back
He's a real pain in the neck!
He's always blowing bubbles with his bubblegum
He loves Coca-Cola
And that's the end of that!
Any takers?

Emma Hoxworth (10)
Bickerton Holy Trinity Primary School

Cinderella

'You shall not exist tomorrow,'
Screamed the prince in terrible sorrow
Cindy peeked from behind the door
She could not watch anymore
Off came the head of the ugly sister
Her face was covered in one big blister
Cindy screamed from the house,
'You horrid thing, you ugly louse.'

Ben Wood (10)
Bickerton Holy Trinity Primary School

MY OWNER PUT ME ON THE TRANSFER LIST

On offer:
One nippy mouse catcher, 5 years old
Caught 10 mice in the freezing cold
Great at home, not much of a pain
Very loving, easy to train
Gets into trouble with any dog
Jumps into ponds following frogs!
This is a free transfer
But he comes with running expenses
Pounds and pounds of Kit-e-Kat
For this very fat cat
He sharpens his claws on your new couch
Snuggles up on your pillow so you can't sleep
Needs a treat once a week
Gets stuck up trees
Does as he pleases
This offer ends at the end of the year
I'll have him back then
To get rid of the mice
Any takers?

Charlotte Archdeacon (10)
Bickerton Holy Trinity Primary School

JUMBLIES

They went to sea in a bin they did,
In a bin they went to sea.
The dolphins in the sea did play,
On a summer's morning on Christmas Day.
In a bin they went to sea
And when the bin got really fast,
The wind did swirl and blew the bin's mast.
They called aloud, 'Our bin ain't much,
We've only got our lazy cat and she's called Fudge!
In a bin we'll go to sea!'

Far and far, far and few,
Are the lands where the Jumblies din,
Their heads are green and their hands are blue
And they went to sea in a bin!

Yanina Morris & Jo Sherwood (9)
Bickerton Holy Trinity Primary School

CINDERELLA

Cindy ran out in her underwear
And lost one slipper on the stair.
The prince picked up the slipper and said,
'Whoever this fits, I will wed.'
In the morning he opened the door,
But sadly we know his luck is quite poor.
The ugly sister tried on the slipper,
To me it looked quite like a flipper.
Then after that, it was Cindy's turn,
It seemed a good fit, it was quite firm.
The prince was happy and shouted, 'Whoopee,
Now this girl will marry me.'
The ugly sisters seemed quite cross,
So the prince showed them who was boss.
'Oh no,' cried the sisters, 'take her away,
We want her back to clean right away.'
The prince chased after her with his bow,
But the dress was ripped from head to toe.
Cindy hopped into the carriage,
Which was in the magic garage.
Cindy rode on into the night,
Until she saw a wonderful sight,
The man of her dreams!

Emma Evans & Jade Hoather (9)
Bickerton Holy Trinity Primary School

MY BROTHER'S PUT ME ON THE TRANSFER LIST!

On offer:
One great artist, eight years old
Has coloured the cat yellow this week
Has a steady hand and an average smile
Knows how to squirt you with paint tubes
Can get sticky and messy within two minutes
Certain to grow out of clothes in three weeks
This is a *free transfer*
But she comes with enormous expenses
Weeks of getting paint out of clothes
Jeans and tops, a box of pens and water colours
Needs to have massive amounts of stencils
Spray paint, pencils and paints
Rubbers, sharpeners, brushes and glue
Endless packets of printer paper
This offer is open until the end of the month
I'll have her back then
At least until the paint's run out
Any takers?

Matthew Dodd (10)
Bickerton Holy Trinity Primary School

MY SISTER'S PUT ME ON THE TRANSFER LIST

On offer:
One brill trampolinist, 13 years old
She jumps so high she sometimes falls
When she comes home, she's always in a mood
She shouts at me when she's eating her food

She comes with shopping expenses
This is a free transfer!
She is quite smart but never shows it
She's mad as could be with her best friend Mel

She's a good long-distance runner
But always shouts back
She only eats junk food, nothing healthy
The worst thing about her is that she annoys me to death
But I think she's the best
Any takers?

Rosie Kendrick (10)
Bickerton Holy Trinity Primary School

MY SISTER'S PUT ME ON THE TRANSFER LIST!

On offer:
One fast runner, eight years old,
Has shot ten birds this year.
He loves walking in the cold,
Likes computers, a TV lover.
Great gymnast, flips fantastic!
Must have trampoline at new home!
Loves pets, especially dogs,
Knows how to get through cat flap.
This is a *free transfer!*
Comes with running expenses,
Must have sausages, hot chocolate, chocolate, crisps,
More sausages, baked beans, home-made bread and then,
Even more sausages.
Cries when he can't get his own way.
Hates school, loves games.
Must have £1.50 every week,
Change of clothes every day,
Endless packets of washing powder.
Offer until the end of the year,
I'll have my brother back then,
At least until the Olympics start.
Anyone dare to take him?

Katie Hunter Johnston (10)
Bickerton Holy Trinity Primary School

MY OWNER'S PUT ME ON THE TRANSFER LIST!

On offer:
One big dog, 6 years old
Has eaten 10,000 bones this season
His coat is gold and he does what he's told
Knows how to beg for his food
His claws are sharp and he knows how to bark
This is a free transfer
But he comes with running expenses
Years of brushing floors and carpets
Shorts and T-shirts and some trousers
Needs to scoff huge amounts of meat
Biscuits and leftovers
Endless packets of doggy treats
This offer is open until the end of the year
I'll have him back then
At least until the dog awards!
Any takers?

James Baker (11)
Bickerton Holy Trinity Primary School

BIG CAT

Giant paws
Massive claws
Big mane
Kills with pain
Some live naturally in the wild
They would eat anything, even a child
They can jump very high
I wonder if they'd like to fly?

Jack Amson (9)
Bickerton Holy Trinity Primary School

HUNGRY BAT

I'm a hungry bat, a staring bat, sucking blood for a drink,
I'm a vampire bat, a sapphire bat, gliding like black ink.
I'm a gliding bat, a hiding bat, eating insects in a cloud,
I love hanging upside-down and have everyone scream so loud.

I'll never eat leaves and grass
And my eyes are the colour of brass.
Not for me the fruit bats
And I love to scare all the rats.

My brass eyes can see in the dark,
I scare the dogs and they start to bark.
I fly around every night
And scare the people, they get such a fright.

Brady Stewart-Chester (10)
Bickerton Holy Trinity Primary School

OWL

I'm a big owl, a furry owl, a barn owl,
  A young owl, a bad fowl!
I'm a sad owl, a mad owl, I glide from side to side,
  There's not another owl to hide.

I'll never be a happy owl, waiting for my food,
  I'm always in a mood.
Not for me is the warm house, nor the cosy seats,
  In my sleep I can hear creaks.

Not for me the cats and rats below,
  I've got a friend, a little crow.
O' my barn is mine alone, the best one yet,
  I'm not an owl for keeping as a pet.

James Hockenhull (9)
Bickerton Holy Trinity Primary School

MY BROTHER PUT ME ON THE TRANSFER LIST

On offer:
One nippy cricketer, seven years old
Has made hundreds of runs this season
Has great handiwork
Knows how to drive a ball
Can score twenty runs in one minute
Guaranteed to help win the game
This is a free transfer
But comes with running expenses
Weeks of washing shirts and trousers, socks
And vests and gloves too
Hundreds of trainers each week
Needs to scoff huge amounts
Of fish, chips, burgers and beans
Pop and Fanta, endless bars of chocolate
This offer is open until the end of the month
I will have him back then
At least until the football starts
Any takers?

Daniel Elder (11)
Bickerton Holy Trinity Primary School

FIGHTER VULTURE

I'm a mean vulture, a team vulture, fighting in the war,
I'm a killer vulture, a thriller vulture, I'd kill today I'm sure.
I'm a sad vulture, a bad vulture, killing for my job,
I only know my workmate and his name's Bob.

Some people think I'm ugly, some think I'm nice,
These people have to die and I'll kill them in a trice.
Not for me the zoo and cage,
I'd rather keep my wild rampage.

Every person that cuts away my home,
It makes no effect, I'll always keep my throne.
Mine is still the best life, with my super knife,
Then I'll just see how I get on with my life.

Gavin Scott (9)
Bickerton Holy Trinity Primary School

JACK FROST

I saw Jack Frost dressed in white,
I couldn't wait to get outside.
The snow was falling,
The clouds were low,
It will soon be Christmas I'll be sad to see it go.

I had my breakfast and got ready,
I couldn't wait to meet my best mate, Freddy.
We made three snowballs and stacked them up high,
We grabbed some coal for Jack Frost's eyes.
We got a carrot for his nose
And some more coal for his mouth and belly,
We got a scarf and hat, he looked pretty smart,
But last of all we got his arms,
We stuck them in and faced them up.

We went to see how Jack Frost was,
He looked happy, he always does.
His hands were cold so we gave him gloves,
'Thanks,' he said, 'thanks a bunch.'
The end of January soon came,
He started melting, what a shame.
'I'll see you next year,' I shouted back.
'The same to you,' I'll soon be back.

Aidan Fraser (10)
Bickerton Holy Trinity Primary School

MY SISTER PUT ME ON THE TRANSFER LIST

One good swimmer, 9 years old,
He got his 50 metres ages ago.
PlayStation, he loves it, don't forget the TV.
This is a *free transfer!*
Stuffs his mouth with sweets,
Comes with endless expenses,
£2.50 pocket money every Friday,
Loves McDonald's,
Spends all his money on toys,
Leaves a *huge* mess in his room.
This offer is open until September,
So he has enough time to buy me a birthday present
If he has any pocket money left!
Any takers?

Robyn Morgan (11)
Bickerton Holy Trinity Primary School

THE BOARDERS

They went down K2 on a surfboard they did,
On a surfboard they went down K2,
In spite of what the Sherpas did,
On the snowy slopes, they saw a big kid,
On a board they went down K2
And when the board span round and round,
Everyone cried, 'You've been re-found.'
They called aloud, 'Our board ain't small,
We don't care a muffin, we don't care a pig.'
Far and few, far and few
Are the lands where the boarders roam,
Their hair is yellow and their boards are red
And they went down K2 on a surfboard.

Ben Hockenhull & Alex Hallam (11)
Bickerton Holy Trinity Primary School

FAT WOLF

I'm a fat wolf, a mean wolf, waiting for my prey,
I'm a crazy wolf, scaring chickens every day,
I hate people, they try to shoot us every week,
I hate daytime, at night I hide-and-seek.

I only ever eat flesh out of chickens and sheep,
I scare everyone, they scream and weep.
I'm only afraid of guns shooting,
I hate the sound of tooting.

I don't like being in a pack,
They put the babies in a sack,
They try to hunt us down,
I hate the noise down town.

Tim Latham (10)
Bickerton Holy Trinity Primary School

THE INK CARTRIDGES

They scuba-dived in a fountain pen,
In a pen they scuba-dived!
In spite of all their inky beds,
The bold captain holding an arrowhead,
In a pen they scuba-dived!
And when the pen began to leak,
They all began to weep,
'Oh no, oh dear,
How stupid we are,
In a pen to scuba-dive!'
Up and under, up and under,
Underneath a hen
Are the lands where the ink cartridges thunder
And they scuba-dived in a pen!

Jack Chandler (10)
Bickerton Holy Trinity Primary School

My Step-Brother Has Put Me On The Transfer List

On offer:
One brilliant chef, nineteen years old
Has won five cooking medals
Has got great skills and a bit of a smile
Knows how to cheat in a competition
Can get food all down him in two minutes
Nearly wrecks his uniform every week
Now this is definitely a *free transfer*
But he comes with a free meal every night
And a week's washed uniforms
Smelly socks and vests, a pair of shoes
Eats pieces of people's leftover food while cooking
Chips, burger, beans, apples, pop and cola
Crisps and oranges and too much gum
This offer is open for ever
I'll have him back one day
At least until the café closes
So, anyone want him?

Jamie Davies (10)
Bickerton Holy Trinity Primary School

My Owner Put Me On The Transfer List

On offer:
One clean cat, 4 months old
Has climbed 40 trees this week
His nifty footwork, nice and neat
Easily dives to his milk and meat
Guaranteed to get dirty in two minutes flat
This is a free transfer
Claws like teeth, chairs are definitely his thing

But he comes with running expenses
Semi-skimmed milk, gold collar and loving 24-7
He will wake you up in the morning
Kids not his thing
This offer is open till the house is finished
Then I'll take him back
Any takers?

Chris Watters (11)
Bickerton Holy Trinity Primary School

MY BROTHER HAS PUT ME ON THE TRANSFER LIST

On offer:
One great pool player, fourteen years old
Has won ten games this season
He has one nifty cue and a big grin
Knows how to snooker anyone, anywhere
Leaves his cues all over the floor
Someday he'll break someone's neck
He's lazy as a slug and as slow as a snail
Guaranteed to wreck his suit every week
This is a definite *free transfer*
But he comes with a free pool table
Weeks of washing shirts and trousers
Socks, vests and pairs of shoes
Needs to scoff huge amounts of McDonald's
Pizza Hut and KFC food
This offer is open until the end of the league
I'll have him back then
At least until the football starts
Any takers?

Jack Cureton (10)
Bickerton Holy Trinity Primary School

My Owner's Put Me On The Transfer List

On offer:
One great lounger, three years old
Has a cute face, sometimes does what he's told
A velvety coat, white with black spots
The only thing is you have to wash him lots and lots
This is a *free transfer*
Weeks of teaching him to sit
He's such a menace, he'll never quit
He eats your homework
He runs away
I really don't know what to say
This offer ends at the start of June
I'll have him back then
As I really will miss him soon
Any takers?

Rosanna Green (9)
Bickerton Holy Trinity Primary School

The Wolf

The wolf is a creature so sleek and mean,
He runs with the wind beneath the moon.

A silent shadow, never to be seen,
He sits on the rock and howls to the dark.

Under a million stars like candles,
He gallops through the midnight forest.

His secret journey almost done,
His cave is waiting, his prize is won.

Mia Geczy (10)
Bickerton Holy Trinity Primary School

MY SISTER PUT ME ON THE TRANSFER LIST

On offer:
A brill rugby player, 18 years old,
Has scored 10 times this season,
He has dislocated his fingers and injured his knee,
He wears cool clothes but gets them mucky,
He's a bit smelly but he has a wash now and then.
This is a free transfer.
Good running expenses,
Piles of washing,
Eats loads of sweets, fruit, chips and pop,
I'll have him back in the summer,
I'd get bored otherwise.
Any takers?

Victoria Sale (11)
Bickerton Holy Trinity Primary School

JUMBLIES

They went to space in a box they did
In a box they went to space
They didn't care what their fans would say
Because they left on a summer's day
In a box they went to space
And when the box began to twirl
Everyone cried, 'You will curl.'
They called aloud, 'Our box is big
But we don't care a fiddle, we don't care a pig
In a box we'll go to space.'
Far and few, far and few
Are the lands where the Jumblies stay
Their bodies are red and their legs are lace
And they went to space in a box.

Laura Raymond (11)
Bickerton Holy Trinity Primary School

THE SNOWMAN

Winter started and the snow came down,
I gave my snowman a little crown.
I saw his eyes as black as night;
And all his body was just white!
All the world was covered in snow;
The worry was that he might go.

The wind picked up and swirled the snow;
My snowman swayed to and fro.
I was frozen like blocks of ice;
A red-hot fire would be nice!
Soon he melted in the snow;
My friend said that he might go.

The poem ends I'm afraid;
I saw my snowman, there he laid.
I couldn't see him anymore;
I went home and closed the door.

Hollie Dempsey (10)
Bickerton Holy Trinity Primary School

CINDERELLA

The prince picks up the battle axe
And takes two almighty whacks.
Off comes the heads, rolling around on the floor,
Coming down the stairs, rolling through the door.
Cindy quietly sitting down,
While the heads are rolling around,
'I can't possibly marry that prince,
He will turn me into mince.'

Ryan Parkes (9)
Bickerton Holy Trinity Primary School

ON OFFER:

One wicked guard dog, 4 years old
He's frightened 4 robbers away cos he's so bold!
He knows how to run and fetch a toy
He leaves muddy footprints, what a naughty boy!
This is a *free transfer*
But to have him you'll be needing money
Weeks of hoovering dog hair
One, two, you're a millionaire!
Needs endless amounts of food
If not, he gets in a mood
Needs walks and lots of attention
Lots of playing with too
This offer is open till someone takes him
How about you?

Rachel Hammond (10)
Bickerton Holy Trinity Primary School

FAT FISH

I'm a fat fish, a flatfish
And I eat from a dish.
I'll sit and make a wish,
That I wasn't a fish.

The fish swim by and make fun of me,
I wonder if I wasn't a fish, what I would be.
I wish I could see
What's out of the sea.

Not for me, the other fish by my side,
They come with me for a short while,
But none will bide.

Thomas Hockenhull (9)
Bickerton Holy Trinity Primary School

THE TISSUES!

They went to space in a tissue box,
In a box they went to space,
In spite of all their bossy friends,
They went to the moon, round the curvy bends,
In a box they went to space
And when the box smelt like a bin,
They all fell out and jumped back in,
They called aloud, 'Our box may smell,
But we don't care a pebble,
We don't care a shell.'
Far and few, far and few
Are the lands where the tissues stock,
Their heads are white and their hands are too
And they went to space in a box!

Charlotte Evans & Camilla Green (11)
Bickerton Holy Trinity Primary School

CINDERELLA

The prince picked up the battle axe
And took two almighty whacks.

Cindy peeked from behind the door,
She said, 'I'm not going to marry him anymore.'

'Who are you, you torn-up trout?
Off with your head,' I have to shout!

The fairy came and went swish, swish,
'Now my dear, you can make a wish.'

Adam Hodgson (9)
Bickerton Holy Trinity Primary School

FLUFFY AND THE TRAPDOOR

Harry, Ron, Hermione,
Flying high to get the key,
Ronald panics and plays chess,
While Harry goes on through the quest,
To search for the locked-up door.

Hermione stays to help her friend,
So Harry starts to the end.
Ron and Hermione have had enough
And all of a sudden they hear a gruff.

It comes from under the cobwebbed door,
They're very scared, that's for sure,
The things they hear are very queer,
The noises are so very near.

Harry wakes up and he's very shocked,
Thinking the cobwebbed door had been locked,
But he soon found out he'd saved the stone,
Suddenly he hears a groan . . .

Kate McKenzie (10)
Bickerton Holy Trinity Primary School

VOLCANO

Had I lived in a volcano of golden lava and silver rocks,
I would spend all my days hunting for a bronze-coloured fish.
Gliding through the lava,
But I, being humble,
I would give it to you with all my heart,
I shall only give you the best fish I can find,
So please keep it as safe as a diamond.

Christopher Alliston (10)
Christchurch Primary School

FIRE!

Fire races through the town,
Hot as lava,
Desperate to destroy,
Creeping, creeping.

Inside the house,
Fingers reaching out,
Towards the living,
Monstrous mouth,
Screaming, shouting.

Creeping, creeping,
Down the street,
Golden arms,
Leading the way.

Voice like thunder,
Intention to kill,
Shifting from side to side,
Creeping, creeping.

Hannah Trousdale (10)
Christchurch Primary School

I AM A BOMB

I am a bomb,
Falling, falling,
Through the sky,
Reaching to kill,
Crash, bang, fire,
Suddenly a building,
Engulfed with flames,
Burning, burning.

Daniel Carter (10)
Christchurch Primary School

When I Grow Up

When I grow up
I would like to be
the master of all poetry.

When I grow up
I would like to be
the keeper of all jewellery.

When I grow up
I would like to be
the lord of all the navy.

When I grow up
I would like to be
a hero who makes people free.

When I grow up
I would like to be
me!

Andrew Arathoon (9)
Christchurch Primary School

V2 Bomb

Quickly bombs fly from the sky,
Into the house, up the town,
Looking and laughing at us,
Quickly the bomb falls from the sky,
Kill, kill is what I do,
Quickly I see a fire around me,
Fire-face bombs in eyes,
Delighted to kill, I am a killer,
Quickly the bombs fall.

Rachel Davies (10)
Christchurch Primary School

FIRE

In the darkness a spark appears,
Deep inferno eyes,
Crawling, crawling.
Its lava tongue licks the air,
Molten mouth eating its prey,
Demon thirsty for blood,
Crawling, crawling.
Furnace flapping arms feeling the way,
Desperate demolisher murdering like mad,
Crawling, crawling.
Infidelity of death,
Possessed by an evil curse,
Crawling, crawling.

Philip Arathoon (10)
Christchurch Primary School

DIAMOND FISH

Had I lived in a sea of diamond fish filled with love and laughter,
Where fish would sway up and down calling your name,
Their silky skin would glisten in the water like diamonds,
They would light up and guide you the way to your heart.

I would send it away in my finest golden paper,
Which would be filled with my love that will last forever.

But being so unfortunate, I can only give away to the poor
My love and laughter which I hope will fill their hearts with tears.

So please care for them as much as you can
And make their lives as happy as can be.

Amanda Parker (10)
Christchurch Primary School

OUT OF THIS WORLD

Had I the whole universe full of love and the stars shining
like diamonds,
Comets that rush to Earth like a horse running to me,
I would give it to you in a box of light
And it would brighten the world with love.
But I, being poor, give you the most precious thing to me –
My family, the most precious thing to me.
I can only give you my dreams, full of love,
So please look after them, look after them please.

Kathryn Stanley (11)
Christchurch Primary School

PARADISE HEAVEN

Had I a paradise island that stretched all over the world,
Stored with all my love that I possess in my heart,
I would give it to you on the finest sea,
But I, being poor and humble,
I can only give you all my trust and love,
So please store it in your most precious part of your heart.

Andrew Banks (11)
Christchurch Primary School

HAD I A CORAL REEF

Had I a coral reef filled with gold and beautiful creatures,
I would give it to you in a precious bubble floating across the sea,
But I, being old and humble,
Can only give my dreams, full of colour and happiness,
So please preserve them inside you, forever.

Ryan Bedwell (11)
Christchurch Primary School

HAD I . . .

Had I a land of bouncy, pink candyfloss
With houses made of ice cream which is warm
And will never melt,
I would give it to the neediest person on Earth,
But I, being humble and poor, I cannot.
I can only give you my dreams,
I dream of rich and beautiful things,
But you are never to sell them.
Please keep them safe in the corner of your deep blue eye
For evermore.

Chloe Green (10)
Christchurch Primary School

SHINING STARS

Had I the stars,
I would send them down to you,
But I, being needy, could not have this,
I can only give my dreams,
So please look after them for me.

Steven Carr (11)
Christchurch Primary School

DEVOTION

Had I a land of devotion which could be cherished forever,
I would give to you with all my strength,
But I, as poor as I am, cannot give you this delightful gift,
But I only give all of my dreams that fulfil my life to you,
So please keep this locked up in your heart.

Laura May Page (10)
Christchurch Primary School

BUBBLEGUM CHOCOLATE

Had I a land of bubblegum chocolate,
Floating in the sky,
I would give it to you from my heart,
But I have no land of bubblegum chocolate,
So I'll give you my hopes and dreams,
So please take care of my hopes and dreams.

Sean Clare (11)
Christchurch Primary School

THE MOUNTAIN

Had I a mountain wrought with gold,
I would send it to you in a fascinating crystal ball,
But I, being poor and in want,
Can only give my most precious dreams
Wrapped in a rag, tag cloth,
So please treasure them with tender love and care.

Joshua Kavanagh (11)
Christchurch Primary School

THE TANK

With my cannon I blast holes in buildings,
I creep round corners then let my cannon fire at will, at will,
I go slowly, slowly,
Down the street, down the street,
My goal is to destroy,
I don't get sleepy.

Daniel Hughes (11)
Christchurch Primary School

WINTER

W is for children wrapping up in bobble hats
I is for black ice and people slipping
N is for naughty children throwing snowballs
T is for parents telling children to be careful
E is for everyone buying scarves
R is for everyone having really good dreams of the summery sun.

Lauren Caldwell (10)
Christchurch Primary School

WINTER

W inter is frosty and icy
I t's time to get our sledges out
N ever-ending snow, cold and fun
T ime to come in from the cold
E veryone in the snow whilst I am having cocoa
R oaring log fires to keep us warm
   I love winter.

Jonathon Revell (9)
Christchurch Primary School

SUMMER

S trappy sandals, sleeveless tops
U tterly lovely barbecues
M arvellous icy lemonade, fine for sweltering sun
M aking sandcastles with buckets and spades
E veryone on holiday
R oasting summer, passing butterflies.

Jessica Birt (10)
Christchurch Primary School

PALACE AND LOVE

Had I a palace, which is mine forever and is filled with peace and love,
I would send it to you wrapped up, in gold wrapping paper,
But I, who have no money, all that I have is love
And dreams to fill your heart,
I will only give all my dreams that I have,
Floating through my head and all my love that I have for you,
So please look after all my love
And all of my dreams that I have sent to you
From my own heart to yours.

Chloe Bebbington (10)
Christchurch Primary School

THE REAL STORY OF . . . RED RIDING HOOD

Red Riding Hood was rather smart
She took her grandmother a red jam tart
And when a wolf got closer
She said, 'Stay back or I will chop off your head.'
When she got to her grandma's house
She chopped the head off a mouse
Called Ned, in bed
She gave the tart to her grandma
But it was then she realised it was not her grandma
It was the wolf from the forest
Aha, I've got him
I'll get him now
Normally in this situation Red Riding
Would whip a pistol from her knickers
But in this case she clobbered him with her Kickers!

Becci Heath (10)
Gorse Hall Primary School

DOGS, DOGS

Dogs, dogs here and there
Dogs, dogs everywhere
Dogs have claws
Dogs have paws
Some dogs run free
Some dogs can't see
Dogs can be sweet
Dogs eat meat
Some dogs have names
Some dogs play games
Dogs can be clever
Some dogs are not clever
Some dogs play football
Some dogs dance in the hall
Dogs, dogs everywhere
Dogs, dogs don't dare to stare
Dogs, dogs, here and there
Dogs, dogs love bones
Dogs, dogs love their homes.

Sophie Whittaker (11)
Gorse Hall Primary School

I KNOW A GIRL

I know a girl,
who is called Pearl.

She eats a lot of meat
and she has *smelly feet.*

Her work is a pity,
but she is pretty.

Adrienne Taylor (8)
Gorse Hall Primary School

TRAINERS

I like my trainers!
In fact they are never off my feet.

I watch the reflectors in the night,
When I'm walking up the street.

They walk some miles, my trainers do,
Footy, shopping and all the way to school.

If I get them muddy,
My mum isn't too impressed.

When I step in doggy-do,
Then she gets very depressed.

Once they're scrubbed up nice and clean,
They are looking cool and mean.

I like my trainers,
Yes I do!

Evan Galloway (11)
Gorse Hall Primary School

DAFFODIL MAGIC

Daffodils, daffodils will only come,
In the light of the sun.
Daffodils are very pretty,
Everyone likes them - even my kitty.

Daffodils will grow anywhere,
As long as you give . . .
Tender loving care.

Chloe Troy (8)
Gorse Hall Primary School

THE HARE AND THE TORTOISE

Once upon a time
In the land of rhyme
A tortoise was sewing
And a mower was mowing
The mower was pushed by a hare who thought himself ace
He challenged the tortoise to a race
The very next day the race went on
But the tortoise had already gone!
Cos at the start
He let out a whopping fart!
He flew a mile
For a while
But the hare was clever, the hare was smart
He dug a tunnel from the start
It came right up out of the ground
Where hare slept without a sound
The tortoise came and drew out a gun
And loaded it with bullets for fun
Bang! Bang! Bang! Hare was dead
50 bullets in his head
The tortoise walked on and won the race
And in the papers was his face
That night he used the hare's carcass to try
A lovely tasting rabbit pie.

Thomas Manson & Shaun Evans (11)
Gorse Hall Primary School

LIGHTNING

Blood punches through every vein
As lightning strikes the windowpane,
Different things happen as a village comes to light.

Lorna Davenport (7)
Gorse Hall Primary School

Bumble Tumble

Bumble tumble
Boil and bubble
Itchy nose
And tickly toes
Mother's leg
On a washing peg
People's arms
Waving for charms
Owl's eye
Always fly
Child's ear
And Dad's tear
Lots of lips
And tiny bits
Everyone's hair
And a big fat bear

Rumble tumble
Boil and bubble
Hope this spell
Will take you to *Hell!*
You will be a human
If you never *tell!*

Rebecca Geraghty (11)
Gorse Hall Primary School

Opposites

One sunny day in the middle of the night
Two dead men got up to fight
They both stood back, facing each other
Took their swords and shot each other.

Chelsey Careless (10)
Gorse Hall Primary School

MY SHADOW

I've lost my shadow
Where could it be?
Up a wall or in a tree?
It's definitely not following me

It was here just a second ago
Walking, jumping to and fro
Have you found someone else
Or got sick of me already?
Because without you shadow, I'm not steady

But shadow where could you be?
Maybe in that pond I see?
There you are shadow
I've found you at last
In the pond, taking a bath . . .

Hannah Griffin (10)
Gorse Hall Primary School

MY FISH

My fish were gold and brown,
One had a little frown.
Their names were Pluto and Dale,
Pluto looked very pale.
I was very sad when they died
And I cried and cried.
Whilst they are dead,
They are still in my head.
I will never forget,
My two tiny pets.

Jack Westwell (9)
Gorse Hall Primary School

SNUGGLE UP

Saturday night, so cold
Snug up right tight,
You might be delighted by
What you dream of tonight.
Morning has arrived
So get up nice and bright,
There's a fresh cup of tea
Waiting to start the day, just right!
Get changed, warm and tight,
Don't forget the shimmery key
To get back in tonight.
When you get home,
The sun is not bright,
Time to snuggle back down,
For the night!

Emily Ormrod (10)
Gorse Hall Primary School

MY BROTHERS

Me and my brothers, that makes three,
We love to climb up a tree.
Taylor, Spencer, Carter, are our names,
We love to play lots of silly games.
Hide-and-seek, duck, duck, goose,
Tying up Spence, so he has to get loose.
Carter likes to play football,
But he always ends up in a fall.
Whatever we do, we always get mucky
And when we come in, my mummy says, 'Yucky!'

Taylor Yates (6)
Gorse Hall Primary School

JACK AND THE BEANSTALK

Jack lived with his humble mother
And a cow, there's no other.
Daisy was the moo-cow's name,
Selling the cow was Jack's aim.
He sold it for a measly bean,
Baked bean shaped and the colour green.
He took it home and showed his mum,
She gave him a kick up the bum.
She threw the bean out the door
And then went and smacked him more.
With no supper he was sent to bed,
Still his bottom was glowing red.
The next morning when he awoke,
He and his mum barely spoke.
He looked out the window and screamed,
It was the beanstalk like he dreamed.
He told his mum and climbed up it,
He lost his breath and had to spit.
At the top he saw a house,
1000 times bigger than a mouse.
It was as big as a cliff,
All the walls straight and stiff.
He went in and saw a giant,
Who seemed to Jack to be a tyrant.
He jumped into his drawer and then,
Took out a golden egg-laying hen.
The hen went cluck, the giant roared,
Jack pulled out his father's sword.
You killed my dad, you won't kill me,
He stood as fierce as he could be.
It didn't work, it was no use,
Jack had to show the flag of truce.

In that moment the giant looked behind,
A spot of luck Jack managed to find.
Down the beanstalk Jack dived,
At the bottom he soon arrived.
Out of the shed Jack took a rocket launcher
And blew the giant to the yet-to-be discovered planet, Crauncher.
From this day on, for evermore,
Jack was rich, never poor.
But this isn't how the story ends,
Here's a fact to tell your friends.
Jack wasn't a chooser, he was a taker,
He married a simple matchstick maker.
After a year he wanted a divorce,
He married a wealthy lawyer of course.

Daniel Love (10)
Gorse Hall Primary School

MY COUSIN, LAURA

My cousin, Laura is bigger than me
She can pick me up quite easily
Laura sometimes sleeps at my house
When she's asleep she's quiet as a mouse
When we are playing hide-and-seek, she always peeks
She's always jealous of my Winnie the Pooh
I don't know if she likes Roo too
My cousin, Laura likes spaghetti
I wonder if she knows Betty?
Laura has got blonde hair
If you meet her, please

Beware!

Amy Miller (9)
Gorse Hall Primary School

MY FRIENDS

I had a little flower, 1, 2, 3,
It was red and shiny just like me.

I had a little pony, I rode it up and down,
I took it to my grandma's and rode it down the town.

I had a little doll, her name was Molly
And she had a friend called Polly.

I took them to the park and soon it was getting dark,
So we ran all the way home.

I had a little cat and one day it ate my hat,
It was black and furry
Its name was Purry
And its second name was Curly.

Abbie Sanderson (6)
Gorse Hall Primary School

CHINESE NEW YEAR

Dashing, dancing through the street
Red and yellow scaly feet
Happy new year has just begun
Giggling children having fun
Happy new year, welcome in
Roaring dragon prancing in.

Walking, talking through the street
Brown and white sandal feet
Back to school has just begun
No laughing children having fun.

Melissa Pearse (11)
Gorse Hall Primary School

THE MAGIC BOX
(Based on 'Magic Box' by Kit Wright)

I will put in my box
The spice of the hottest pepper,
A scale from the midnight dragon,
The light of the evening moon.

I will put in my box
A spark from a winter fire,
The blood of a rare unicorn
And the leaves falling off an autumn tree.

I will put in my box
Purple violets growing in a field,
Fire from a flying phoenix
And the breeze of the southern wind.

My box is fashioned from gold, pearls and rubies,
With light and piece of the burning sun on the bright lid.

I shall travel in my box,
Explore the jungle and woods of the Earth,
Also the blue sea gently touching the yellow sand
Of God's beaches.

Jonathan Hand (10)
Gorse Hall Primary School

FAT CAT

There once was a cat who lived on a mat
And was as lazy as my dad
He never got up for any meals
But he was still fat
The fat cat who lived on a mat.

Hannah Taylor (7)
Gorse Hall Primary School

I CAN SEE YOU, DUCKY

I can see you, Ducky,
You are very lucky,
You need a friend,
On me you can depend.

I can see you, Ducky,
She is white,
She is pale,
She has got a shiny tail.

Jenny Laing (7)
Gorse Hall Primary School

LOVE

Love is a bright glossy red,
It smells like red roses in the garden,
Love tastes like the strawberry chocolate,
It sounds like the human heart beating,
It feels like smooth petals on a flower,
It lives in the heart of two people.

James Rowbotham (10)
Gorse Hall Primary School

TEETH

Teeth are clean, teeth are white
Keep them healthy by brushing them right
Get the right toothpaste, get the right brush
Take your time, no need to rush

Brush them up, brush them down
Try not to frown, don't look down
Teeth are clean, teeth are white
Keep them healthy by brushing them right.

Lilly Selwood (7)
Gorse Hall Primary School

TEDDY BEAR

Teddy bear, teddy bear
Where are you?
Teddy bear, teddy bear
Down the loo!
Teddy bear, teddy bear
What can you see?
Teddy bear, teddy bear
A monkey looking at me.

Amanda Brooks (8)
Gorse Hall Primary School

TEN LITTLE FINGERS

Ten little fingers jump up and down,
Ten little fingers go to town.
Ten little fingers play all day,
Ten little fingers hide away.

Jordan Elliott (6)
Gorse Hall Primary School

CHRISTMAS

C hristmas is a happy time,
H aving loads of food and drink,
R aping music, fun and games,
I always shout, 'Are these mine?'
S anta always comes to me, never lets me down,
T urkey is the main meal,
M y friends come all the time,
A ll I want to say is . . .
S anta, thank you.

Luke Barlow (9)
Gorse Hall Primary School

SADNESS

Sadness is navy-blue
It smells like salty water
It feels like wet sand
Sadness tastes like lemon juice
It sounds like waves crashing against rocks
Sadness lives in your tears, falling down your face.

Hayley Lawlor (10)
Gorse Hall Primary School

STAR

Shining brightly in the sky,
When it is dark at night
It sparkles with the moon,
When the sun starts to rise,
It fades away like a dying rose.

Abbie Broadhead (7)
Gorse Hall Primary School

TEDDY BEAR, TEDDY BEAR

Teddy bear, teddy bear where are you?
Teddy bear, teddy bear you've caught the flu.
Teddy bear, teddy bear eat your cheese,
Teddy bear, teddy bear you've got the fleas.
Teddy bear, teddy bear eat your dinner,
Teddy bear, teddy bear you look thinner.
Teddy bear, teddy bear come out to play,
Teddy bear, teddy bear you've brightened my day.

Megan Partington (8)
Gorse Hall Primary School

NOW I'M GONE

I feel so warm
But feel so cold
I need you here
For me to hold
The tears I cry
Are all for you
Now I'm gone
I love you.

Christopher Layton (11)
Gorse Hall Primary School

TEN LITTLE TODDLERS

Ten little toddlers go to the park,
Ten little toddlers pretend to bark.
Ten little toddlers dance all day,
Ten little toddlers hide away.

Christina Bradbury (6)
Gorse Hall Primary School

IF . . .

(In dedication to my grandad, George Wild)

If my grandad was a tree,
he'd be a chestnut tree on the smooth green grass.

If my grandad was an animal
he'd be a monkey playing jokes and being funny.

If my grandad was a fruit
he'd be a soft orange.

If my grandad was the weather
he'd be the shining summer sun.

If my grandad was a piece of furniture
he'd be a soft armchair.

If my grandad was an instrument
he'd be a noisy trumpet.

If my grandad was a beer
he'd be a pint of Boddingtons.

If my grandad was a colour
he'd be red for roses.

If my grandad was a piece of clothing
he'd be a soft, woolly jumper.

If my grandad was a flower
he'd be a beautiful rose.

If my grandad was a pop star
he'd be Tom Jones!

Kayley Sanderson (10)
Gorse Hall Primary School

BONFIRE NIGHT

The fire is bright,
On Bonfire Night,
The flames reach up to the sky,
Going up, up, up so high.

They leap and dance,
Crackle and prance.
The people watch the light,
Screaming with delight.

Now the fireworks pop and fizz
And sometimes they will screech and whizz.

Twisting and turning,
Whistling and whirling.
Screaming and screeching,
Always reaching,
Up towards the sky.

Treacle toffee,
Sometimes coffee.
Potatoes roasting,
I am toasting
By the fire, so hot.

Now the fire is dying down
And all the twigs are brown.
The food and fireworks
Are all gone,
And now the night is done.

David Ashworth (9)
Hursthead Junior School

MY FAVOURITE THINGS

Hot yorkshire puddings with beef and gravy
My hair after plaiting, all shiny and wavy
Crunchy white snow on a wintry day
Fairies in stories who dance and play
Glittery gel pens that smell sweet and fruity
The magical tale of fair Sleeping Beauty
Twinkling stars which sparkle and shine
Cool fizzy water with lemon and lime
Singing along to some pop music songs
Sticking my nose into books that are long
Teasing my brain with puzzles and sums
Helping my mum to bake biscuits and buns
Sunshine and swimming which holidays bring
These are some of my favourite things.

Chloe Edmonds (8)
Hursthead Junior School

FAVOURITE THINGS

Watching gorillas at the zoo,
Scorching summer sand,
Tasty chicken and gravy,
Scoring goals at football,
The excitement of Christmas,
Playing under water,
Hearing my little sister saying funny words,
Making a snowman,
Watching dazzling fireworks exploding in the night sky,
Laughing with my friends,
Walking in the park with Grandpa.

Thomas Proffitt (8)
Hursthead Junior School

HENRY ON THE BALL

Henry has a very powerful shot on the ball
And he has got good pace
When he does a fantastic curl, it goes in the back of the net
When Viera takes a corner
Henry jumps up and scores with his strong head
When he does a fast dribble down the wing
He does a hard turn and takes someone on
And does a crisp pass to Bergkamp and Bergkamp scores
He has a nice, smart French accent
And some nice shining boots
And massive muscles on his thighs
To make him run faster.

Patrick Fripp (9)
Hursthead Junior School

MY SPECIAL CAT

My special cat
Is soft and slim
Furry and fluffy she is
She's my favourite cat
Half-Persian half-tabby
She's soft and cuddly too
Slinking slowly across the grass
Brushing herself on the bushes
Her bottlebrush tail swaying in the air
My special cat says goodnight to me always
Whispering her way across the carpet
To spring on my bed for a fuss.

Holly Bassett (8)
Hursthead Junior School

MY DAY OUT WITH DAD

My dad supports a football team,
Swansea City, they're a scream.
Bottom of Division Three,
A sadder sight you'll never see.

What better on a Saturday,
Than head to Macc to see them play.
We met Dad's mate in the pub,
Drinking beer and eating grub.

The match was great, it was a blast,
Swansea scored the goals too fast.
The ref was fat, bald and a cheat,
So slow I thought he had bare feet.

The win went to Swansea City,
MT one SC three,
My dad was pleased, it made his day,
Swansea never win away.

Jack Llewellyn (8)
Hursthead Junior School

MY DOG, BOB

My dog, Bob is a very good boy,
He likes to run and chase his soft toy,
He loves to dig in the sand and swim in the sea
And when he gets home, he gobbles his tea,
At the end of the day, when we've all gone to sleep,
Off to his basket Bobby will creep.

George Ramsden (8)
Hursthead Junior School

CAVES

In the dark, scary caves
You can hear;
The bats swooping, swishing around
And the rats scurrying, hurrying around, until
Pound
The bats eat the rats.
Up high around the stalagmites and stalactites
You can see the gigantic cobwebs
And spiders
And again
Pound
The bats get the spiders.
Oh my word, what a fat bat
Oh no!
Help! The bats are coming to eat me
Arrgghh!
I hurry outside as fast as I can
I see the light and bright sun and green grass;
I am saved
What a frightening nightmare it was
How delightful to be safe again!

Joe Forooghian (9)
Hursthead Junior School

THE BIG MATCH

I play for a football team, they are my local club,
They are called Mountfield Rovers.
We played a match at our home pitch against Woodley,
We won the match 8-0.
Three players scored, one was James Huxley.

James Huxley (9)
Hursthead Junior School

MY DOG, RUFUS

He's not fat
He's not small
He's in-between that's all

Big, bushy eyebrows,
White whiskers and a beard,
I think he is cute
Some people think he's weird

A coat like chocolate
A nose like fudge
But when he sits on your knee
He just won't budge

Springy and bouncy
But not at all grouchy
A little bit smelly
Sometimes like an old welly

He's my best pal
He sleeps on my bed
He starts to snarl when I stroke his head

That's my dog alright
And he's the best.

Jamie Elms (8)
Hursthead Junior School

HOLIDAYS

Holidays are lots of fun
When you have melting hot sun
Swimming and football are the best
It's even nice to have a rest (from school!)

I went to Devon with my uncle Kevin
I've been to France, just by chance
Camping in Wales was a little bit cold
I'll go to Florida when I am ten years old.

Douglas Miller (8)
Hursthead Junior School

MY FAVOURITE THINGS

Of all the things I like the best
My favourite is sport, it beats the rest
At football I score lots of goals
At cricket, batsmen fear my balls
And with a bat I score the run
To make sure the game is won
And with a rugby ball I fly
Down the wing to score a try
I like cross-country and run for the school
Sport is great, it's really cool!

Daniel Rothel (7)
Hursthead Junior School

SNOW LEOPARD

A snow leopard runs and prances
So graceful, it looks like it dances
They look cute and fluffy
But they're big and fierce
They sleep in trees
And crawl on their knees
To hunt down their prey
And eat where they lay.

Melanie Askew (9)
Hursthead Junior School

FOOTBALL

Football is my passion
It drives my mum round the bend
I play it every day
Could there possibly be an end?

I play it on my PlayStation
With a group of my best friends
The room gets very noisy
My sister's hair stands on end!

On Saturdays I go training
We hope the pitch is green
But usually it isn't
So thank goodness for the washing machine

Football is my passion
And I hope that one day
People will go to Edgeley Park
To watch me and my team play.

Adam Sedgwick (8)
Hursthead Junior School

FOOTBALL

F   ans cheering you on when you've got the ball
O   n the coach going to the football match
O   ffside signals the assistant referee
T   umbling down dreadful challenge
B   all getting kicked about, great passing
A   mazing goal kick, it went flying
L   obbed the keeper, brilliant goal
L   ost, oh no!

Daniel Wheatley (9)
Hursthead Junior School

MY FAVOURITE THINGS

I love my rabbit, Fluffy
She's cuddly, soft and cute
She likes to munch on carrots and leaves
But apples are her favourite fruit.

It's fun going on a bike ride
I like to go very fast
Michael sits on the back of Dad's bike and shouts,
'Hurry, let's blast past.'

I love going on holiday
I like the beach and pool
When I've been playing in the sun
An ice cream keeps me cool

I like going on the computer
My Spy Fox game is fun
When I've finished I shout,
'Mum, Dad, I'm done.'

Jessica Armstrong (7)
Hursthead Junior School

MY FAVOURITE THINGS

My favourite things all have wings,
Cuckoos like to whistle and the nightingale sings.
Aeroplanes soar up in the sky,
While the bees zoom through the sky
Looking for pollen as they drop by.
Dragonflies hover above watery ground,
Whilst the butterflies flutter without a sound.
My favourite are bats, which zip and swoop,
As they fly in the night.

Lauren Williams (7)
Hursthead Junior School

A Recipe For A Snowman

Open a large tin of snow and heat it until it's runny,
Then put it into your bowl.
Take a sack of coal and stick two pieces of coal into your mix,
Then get a collection of stones and put six stones into your bowl.
When that's done, get a scarf and marinade it in water overnight
And put it into the bowl.
Then get a carrot and roast it and put that in the mix.
Then get a hat and freeze it and add it to the mix.
Then get some sticks and roast them and add them to the bowl.
Then get a pipe and decorate it and put it in the bowl
And get some gloves and stir-fry them and put them in.
Then get some buttons and put them in the mix
Stir and freeze the mix and leave it for a night
And you will find a snowman!

Sophie Goodlass (7)
Hursthead Junior School

A Recipe For A Beach

Get a packet of shells and grind them into bits
Then chop some fish and add it to the mixture
Then get a bucket of waves and spread it over the mixture
Next, get a surfboard and chop it into small pieces
And add them to the mixture
Then boil your mixture with candyfloss for half an hour
Take it out and sprinkle with sand
Leave it for 5 minutes
Then get a tub of ice cream and squash it into the mixture
Take a starfish and with a sharp knife
Chop off the sharp bits and add it to the mixture
Decorate with sweets
And your beach is ready.

Travis Heywood (7)
Hursthead Junior School

THE FOOTBALL MATCH

Sitting in the stadium, waiting for the match to start,
The music's loud, the fans cheering their teams to play their part.
The football pitch is huge, with lines and goals at each end,
The floodlights are on, the scoreboard lit, to show the balls that bend
Into the goals, the crowd will cheer because their team has scored,
It's much more fun being at the match than sitting at home bored.

The players on the substitute bench all jump around with glee,
The other team's players are not happy and they approach the referee.
The managers sit there worried, their jobs are on the line,
The coach looks at his watch and the whistle goes for time.
The competition is over, my team has won again,
My spirits are high but my clothes are wet,
I've been standing in the rain.

Christian Cook (8)
Hursthead Junior School

NIGHT STARS

In the deep darkness of the night
Glittering stars glow a golden glow
They shimmer light upon the ground
Shooting stars make streams of colour
The trail of glimmering colour
Simmers slowly to the soft ground
The dazzling golden stars
Hang among the pitch-black sky
Like sparkling flowers of ice
They glitter and shimmer
Above the darkness
In space
Night stars.

Carolyn Luo Ward (9)
Hursthead Junior School

GREEDY DOG

Greedy dog eating all day
Greedy dog no time to play
Only time for eating and sleeping
Lies with his eyes under paws a-peeping

Greedy dog met a fat cat
Fat cat was black and white and wearing a hat
Fat cat went off a-hunting
Only to find a huge amount of bunting

Fat cat met a mouse
In a house
The mouse ran along a log
Only to find the greedy dog.

Hannah McBride (8)
Hursthead Junior School

MY PET

My pet dog
Can turn into a frog
A rabbit or a hog
Because he's an imaginary dog

He lives in my house
And is as quiet as a mouse
He doesn't eat very much
And he is difficult to touch

My mum doesn't know
So he'll never have to go
He is my friend
Until the end.

Josh Atkinson (8)
Hursthead Junior School

MY BROTHER'S BEAR

My brother's bear, Alfie
Goes everywhere
He takes him to bed
And thinks he's real
He even takes him out
For a meal!
My brother's bear goes
Everywhere!

He goes on holiday
And out in the car
On our family photo
He was the shining star
For Heaven's sake
It's no mistake
He goes absolutely
Everywhere!

Scott Cockerham (8)
Hursthead Junior School

LIVERPOOL

L   iverpool are my team
I   like them very much
V   ladimir Smicer is number seven
E   very week he's in the team
R   iise plays at number eighteen
P   lease say they'll win the league
O   wen is my hero
O   nly he can win a match
L   iverpool rule
    OK!

Alice Kaiser (8)
Hursthead Junior School

MORAL DECHANT

Think my people, of all those here,
Homeless, often clotheless, I feel so bad,
Can't we do a thing to help?
It's just not fair.

I mean, think of all the different people,
Different ages, young and old,
Short, long and thin,
All are sleeping on a hard brick wall,
Which would make you or I catch cold
And here, we relax in luxury,
It's just not fair.

By working with a charity,
We can make the fact disappear,
Give them food and clothing too,
Then it's fair.

Ellen Powell (9)
Hursthead Junior School

FRIENDSHIP

F   riends forever
R   eally good times
I   n the park we like to play
E   very day we meet each other
N   ever-ending laughter
D   ifferent games every day
S   haring sweets and other things
H   elping each other when they're hurt
I   mportant to have
P   erfect friendship.

Bethany Simpson (9)
Hursthead Junior School

MY FAVOURITE THINGS

Action things are what I like
Most of all to play
Especially on my PS2
I could sit there all day

Another thing I really like
Is eating fish and chips
With salt and vinegar and red sauce
I can taste them on my lips

So many things that I enjoy
But often as a rule
The thing that I like most of all
Is being really cool!

Jonathan Cresswell (8)
Hursthead Junior School

ROCK 'N' ROLL

You've got to try and fly
Up into the sky,
Even if you're scared or shy.

You go up the ramp,
Then do a grind,
Who cares if someone
Is close up behind.

You've got to try and try,
One day you'll be able to fly
Up into the sky,
You won't be scared or shy.

Georgia Newman (9)
Hursthead Junior School

MY FAMILY

In my family I have . . .
A cheeky little sister
She sends me round the bend
In my family I have . . .
A strong dad
He's as loveable as a puppy
But when we're a little bad
It makes him feel inside sad
In my family I have . . .
Last,. but certainly not least
My fabulous mum
She's great in all ways
But best of all
She loves us with all her heart!

Jessica Mostyn (8)
Hursthead Junior School

YOUNG BROTHERS

Young brothers are very annoying
and enjoy a lot of chocolate.
They eat and eat and eat it,
they fight and fight and fight me,
I try not to kick him
but he kicks me anyway
and I try to be nice
but he'll just be nasty to me all the time.
It's hard to have a little brother.
Oh yes!
But, you know what?
I'll always love my brother!

Robert Hart (8)
Hursthead Junior School

CHOGALA

The chogala has 49 heads
And when he catches a cold (which he hates)
He has 49 noses to blow

The chogala has 40 arms
Which is very good
If you have lots of jobs

The chogala has 60 legs
Which is good for walking long distances

The chogala is a monstrous beast
And I'm glad I've never met him!

Sophie McCarthy (9)
Hursthead Junior School

GIRLS

Girls, girls
Don't forget
They are better
Than the rest
Boys, boys
Ugly boys
Might mighty
Yeah right
Chant
Girls are the best
As what the truth is
Girls are the best
Boys may be the rest.

Melissa Matos (8)
Hursthead Junior School

SANDCASTLE

S   un is shining in the sky
A   nd the sand is hot
N   ow's the time to start digging
D   o something new at the beach today
C   rabs scuttle around you
A   nd there are fish in the sea
S   hells to decorate your sandcastle
T   he tide is coming in
L   ight breezes make the flag flutter
E   nd of the day, it's time to go home
     Bye-bye sandcastle, I won't see you again.

Hannah Simpson (9)
Hursthead Junior School

RABBITS

Rabbits are soft,
Rabbits are sweet,
Rabbits are awesome,
Rabbits can be tiny or huge
And some can be fat or slim,
Rabbits can be any colour,
But in any way they'll always be cute.

Autumn Corry (9)
Hursthead Junior School

MY DOG

My dog's name is Cassie,
She's the funniest dog I know,
When I pick up her food bowl
She goes mad till it's full

My dog is so funny when we take her on walks
She runs sideways like a crab with an engine on its back
Cassie is the cutest dog in the world
She is also the funniest dog too.

Anna Carley (9)
Hursthead Junior School

THE GIANT

There once was a giant
A great big ogre
He lived in a dark gloomy cave
Lit with lanterns
Surrounded by cobwebs
The food he enjoys, he will never save
He will gobble it up and lick his dirty fingers
Without any thought he will spit and dribble, crunch and grind
Beware, beware, don't travel near his home
For the giant you will find isn't the pleasant kind!

Luke Daniels (8)
Hursthead Junior School

FIONA, MY PET RABBIT

Fiona's fur is milky-white
Her ears are as soft as snow
My rabbit's eyes are chestnut-brown
When she looks at me it's as if she understands every word I say
If ever I am upset or sad, Fiona's always there to sit beside me
Fiona, Fiona, I don't know what I would do without her.

Sarah Daisy Kirkham (8)
Hursthead Junior School

FOOTBALL CRAZY

I'm football crazy, I'm football mad
I started playing football when I was a little lad
I lined up the shot
Then I curved the ball, it's a goal and it's 10-0
The crowd go wild and cheer
I'm football crazy, I'm football mad
I started playing football when I was a little lad
They take a shot and our goalie saves it
I run down the wing and I score again
I'm football crazy, I'm football mad
I started playing football when I was a little lad.

Alexander Read (8)
Hursthead Junior School

THE DRAGON

The dragon has fire as a mouth,
The dragon has laser eyes; its wings are like tornadoes,
His claws are so sharp they could rip up the world,
His ears are so strong they can hear like a fox,
Do not explore near him,
Beware of the dragon!

Matt Richardson (9)
Hursthead Junior School

MY FISH

In a tiny tank they swim around the blue and green bowl,
Two go one way and the others go the other way I found.

Sparkle and Angel swim together, I think that Sparkle is her daughter,
Side by side they glide through the shimmering, shiny water.

Fire is the dad, the boss and the chief,
Some say that Fred is a big thief!

I love my fish, Fire, Fred, Sparkle and Angel,
I am sure that they all love me too.

Katherine King (8)
Hursthead Junior School

BEE

I have a favourite toy called Bee,
He's the same age as me,
Everything I see and do,
He always sees it with me too,
I lost him on holiday, I was so sad,
But someone found him, I was so glad,
He used to be pink but now he is grey,
Because all his colour has washed away,
He is very scruffy but I don't care,
He will always be my very special bear.

Kate Buxton (7)
Hursthead Junior School

MY LIFE

When I was one, I ate a scone,
When I was two, I learnt to say boo,
When I was three, I climbed a tree,
When I was four, you'll never guess what I saw?
When I was five, I learnt to dive,
When I was six, I ate a Twix,
When I was seven, I went to Heaven.

Benjamin Ashton (9)
Hursthead Junior School

CATS

Cats slink around through dustbins
Finding leftovers
Fighting with other cats

They are lazy cats
And they are playful cats
Or they are holiday cats
But there's one cat I like best
My cat!

Charlotte Gabbitas (8)
Hursthead Junior School

FISHING

I always go fishing with Charles and my dad
We enjoy sitting and watching the float
In the hope a fish will bite
If we catch one, it makes me happy
If not, then we go home.

Max Hartle (7)
Hursthead Junior School

PIANO

P   iano is the best
I   s better than the rest
A   great instrument to play
N   ot the worst
O   f the music family.

Hannah Farrell (8)
Hursthead Junior School

RECIPE FOR A HAUNTED HOUSE

Get a bowl and put some blood in
Mix it well
Add some ghouls
Get some monsters and hang them up
Put a fan behind them
Sprinkle the blood mixture on them
And you have a haunted house.

Aidan Nahirny (7)
Hursthead Junior School

RECIPE FOR A HAUNTED HOUSE

Open a large packet of vampires
Mix it with blood
Leave it to bake for 40 minutes
Then chop up some bats
Sprinkle over the top
Then you have a spooky, haunted house.

Lewis Walls (8)
Hursthead Junior School

I LIKE - YOU LIKE

I like sunshine, you like rain
When you're nice . . .
You make me insane!
I like cats, you like dogs
I'm a girl, you're a boy
Do we like anything the same?

Aimée Mounfield (9)
Hursthead Junior School

My Favourite Things

Splashing in the sea and eating ice cream
Laying on the warm sand and building sandcastles
Warm, sunny days in the garden
Paddling in the paddling pool
Crayoning in pictures with beautiful colours
Rearranging the furniture in my doll's house
Playing on the computer and tunes on the piano
Munching on chewy toffee
Building snowmen from crisp, crunchy snow
Snuggling up warm and watching TV
Baking with my grandma
These are the things I love!

Alexandra Stone (7)
Hursthead Junior School

Football

Football is the greatest game that I have ever seen
Supporters travel throughout the land
To watch their favourite team
The crowd like to sing and chant
To help the players score
And when they do, the crowd all cheer
With such a great big roar
The players wear their kit with pride
Shiny boots and brave inside
Winning is such a treat
Because Man United
Are hard to beat.

Thomas Bolton (8)
Hursthead Junior School

SHARKS

The swishing of the tail
The ripping of the jaws
The rolling black eyes
Sweat runs from your pores

He's coming
And this time it's for you!
Swim away! Out of sight!
So he'll get someone new

The swishing of the tail
The ripping of the jaws
The rolling black eyes
Sweat runs from your pores

He's heading towards you
There's nowhere to run
He's picking up speed
He's going to have some fun

The swishing of the tail
The ripping of the jaws
The rolling black eyes
The sweat runs from your pores

His razor-like teeth tear at your skin
Your silent scream fills the water
He lets go at last
Your leg is suddenly shorter!

The swishing of the tail
The ripping of the jaws
The rolling black eyes
The sweat runs from your pores.

Michael Graham (11)
Hursthead Junior School

MY SCHOOL DAYS

This is a poem about 'my school days',
Which I like and dislike in so many ways.
I arrive at 8.40 ready to go,
Uniform pressed neatly from head to toe.

Monday
Monday pm brings all kinds of things,
Out on the games field, jumping through rings.
Running through mud patches, splashing in rain,
Mum won't be pleased with the washing again.

Tuesday
One day down, only four left to do,
English and maths and perhaps science too.
Playtimes are the best you see,
Because I can play out, my friends and me.

Wednesday
Thank goodness no assembly, just the register to take,
Then change round for maths sets, I must stay awake.
I can't wait for drama, where I learn to mime,
Four o'clock comes quickly, gosh look at the time!

Thursday
Hooray, it's Thursday, to cross-country I go,
To be shouted along, I mustn't be slow.
My face turns all red, like the colour of our vest,
I don't mind because I'm just doing my best.

Friday
Friday, it's the weekend, I feel as high as a kite,
Off to friends' parties, staying the night.
Why does the weekend always go so quick?
I'll borrow Bernard's watch, that'll do the trick!

It has come to the end of this great poem,
It's such a shame we couldn't keep on going.
Pack up your stuff because it's home time!
And I hope you enjoyed my little rhyme.

Melissa Wilkinson (11)
Hursthead Junior School

THE SECRETS OF THE NIGHT

Soulful people wailing, for all of us to hear,
All the drunk men laughing, from drinking wine and beer.
Magical witches cackling, while mixing up a stew,
Old gutter-people crying, for being sucked in goo.

Smell of fires burning, and smoke reaching for the stars,
You can see its shape turn into claws, to catch the birds afar.
Just smell the soothing drinking chocolate, bubbling on the stove
And don't forget that sickly smell of Dad's sweaty, stinky clothes.

There, far in the distance is that mysterious, mystical moon,
Also at hand are celebrations, with all sorts of bright balloons.
There is the flashing lightning, making people freeze in shock,
Oh, there the sad widows, gathering winter stock.

All you can feel is ice-cold wind, brushing against your poor cheeks
And you can feel a sloppy kiss from Mum to say goodnight. Eek!
But then the sleepy monster blows you a midnight dream
And makes you feel so warm inside, it orders you to beam.

That's all of the night's secrets, all of them but one,
But you've always known this secret, you've known it all along.
You say, 'Tell us that secret. Tell us, oh do.'
Alright then. For night loves you!

Ella Bucknall (9)
Hursthead Junior School

BRAMBLE, MY PET RABBIT

Bramble is my pet rabbit,
Just before tea, he comes hopping right up to me.
He's so fluffy that he looks puffy.
He smells of toffee and watches my mum drink her coffee.
He watches United V Man City, what a pity.
He sleeps in his shed, in his comfortable bed.
He sleeps in a bed of straw, licking his paw.
I pick him up and he looks at me like a pup.
He's black and white and curls himself up tight.
When he stretches himself out, he looks like a water spout.
Bramble is gentle, but drives Grandma mental.
I put him in a pen and he looks like a hen.
When he saw himself in the mirror he got quite a fright.
He loves his home for he gets a comb.
I talk to him as if he's a human.
He banged his head on the door when my dog was four.
When a cat sees him, he scares them off and I give him a good pat.
When I first saw him, he was as small as a kitten and he played
                                        with my mitten,
But now when I feed him, he's as big as a mountain.
His eyes are brown while he watches the town.
He is so cute, he makes you want to play the flute.
He ate a pie and wrecked Dad's tie.
His tongue is red as fire.
His favourite food is apples.
He likes to skip to the tip.
He likes to watch TV with me.
I named him Bramble cos he's always getting in a tangle.
Bramble is my pet.

Rebekah Dean (11)
Hursthead Junior School

SPORTING HOBBIES

These are a few of my favourite things
For this is the joy which each of them brings:

Well, firstly there's football, I play by the rules,
I play it at home and also in school,
Manchester United is my favourite team,
There's Beckham, Scholes, Veron and Keane,
My dream is to get on the pitch and play
And I'd like to do that every day.

Next there's rugby, a great team sport,
These are the things you have to be taught,
Running, kicking, passing and tackling,
But at first you might think these are frightening,
To win the game you have to be keen
And this applies to the whole fifteen.

Tennis is another of my favourite sports,
We play in the summer on the Queensgate courts,
Singles are good when I play with my friend,
He tries very hard but I win in the end,
I play every day in the summer term
And all the time there's a new thing to learn.

Finally there's badminton another racket sport,
But this time it's on an indoor court,
You have to hit the shuttle over the net
And if you don't do this, you'll lose the set,
The game is played at such a great speed,
You'll have to be quick to take the lead.

Jack Worne (10)
Hursthead Junior School

RUGBY

Rugby is the sport I play,
With my team on Sunday,
Scoring tries is the aim,
Even if it causes pain,
We tackle hard, rook and maul,
Trying to get our hands on the muddy ball,
Into the scrum, out through their legs,
We run and pass down the line
And hope it will be fine,
Out to the wing, off like a spring,
The speed of light,
Dodge a tackle here and there,
Open run,
Tired out,
A trip,
A fall,
A slip,
A slide,
Over the line,
We've scored a try.

Jack Moores (11)
Hursthead Junior School

RECIPE FOR A PARTY

Take some big balloons
Add some spices
Stir in some happy children
Spread over some potatoes
Sprinkle some nice presents
And grated cheese over the top.

Matthew Bailey (7)
Hursthead Junior School

CASPA

His heavy soft fur coat is a Persian rug
Of bronze and black trees,
Buffeted about like grass in the wind.
Teeth worn down to short stone stumps
Like a donkey's.
Padded paws as soft as the velvet sky at night.
Eyes like the glowing furnace of molten rock
In a volcano as he sits,
Purring as a proud sphinx,
Looking over the familiar desert of the lounge.

His conversational skills consist of curious miaows,
They echo in your mind.
Or the occasional yowl after a family holiday,
'How dare you leave me here on my own!'
Then the comforting purr that greets your ears
When you have a coal-black lion sitting on your lap.
That is the meaning of contentment and happiness.
But, most of all,
The greatest honour
Is having your tired limbs warmed
By a wandering black, long-haired tomcat.

Samuel Bradley (11)
Hursthead Junior School

THE FOREST AT NIGHT

The tree's long, leafy fingers wave round you in shadows,
The owl's hoots screech down your eardrum like knives,
The mouse's scutters sends icy-cold shivers up your spine,
Then you are on your own,
In the cold looming forest at night.

Bethany Williams (11)
Hursthead Junior School

LIFE!

I remember good times
And bad ones too.
I try only to remember good ones,
But bad ones play flashbacks.
I don't like people to hang their heads in gloom,
But to blossom and bloom.
Don't be dull,
Live life to the full.
Have fun in everything you do
And be happy in you.
You can't live life alone,
You need friends and a happy home.
So here's my advice to you,
Don't be dull,
Live life to the full.

Your life means more than just you,
A smile on your face could go a long way.
People need a helping hand in life, including you.
So be nice to everyone you meet
And everyone will be pleased all around.
So don't be dull,
Live life to the full.

Becky Dawson (11)
Hursthead Junior School

MY CAT, HER CAT

My cat is brown, black and white
My cat is always having a fight
My cat is black, blue and red
My cat has bruises on its head
My cat is very rough and tough
My cat is the one I'll always love

Her cat is ginger, brown and white
Her cat never gets into a fight
Her cat has long whiskers upon its head
Her cat has a cotton feather bed
Her cat is soft and cuddly
Her cat is the one that's not for me.

Matthew Kirton (11)
Hursthead Junior School

WEATHER

Rain or shine,
    the weather is fine.
Either way,
    it is OK.

The lightning is frightening,
    the sun is fun.
The thunder's a wonder,
    it sounds like a gun.

Rain or shine,
    the weather is fine.
Either way,
    it is OK.

The snow can come down from high to low,
    the ice is nice, but the cold hurts my toes.
The rain falls down into a drain,
    a gust of wind down the lane.

Rain or shine,
    the weather is fine.
Either way,
it is OK!

Verity Rushton (11)
Hursthead Junior School

CHARLIE

Charlie is very small
Charlie is a dog
Charlie is very cute
Because he's a funny dog

He chases cats all around
He's enough to drive you bonkers
He sniffs all day with his nose
Because he's a funny dog

He takes three walks each day
And he runs around the garden
His favourite toy is a ball
Because he's a funny dog

When he eats his tea
He never leaves a drop
He's very, very cuddly
Because he's a funny dog

He's very nice to everyone
And always does what he is told
He likes to be stroked round the ear
Because he's a funny dog.

Ben Porter (11)
Hursthead Junior School

MY HOBBY

My hobby is playing with my dog
You can sometimes see her chasing a frog
She's sometimes a pain
With a pea as a brain
And her favourite game is getting in the way

I take her for walks
And she tries to talk
About sausages and mash
And potato hash
And then we have to dash home for tea.

Lauren Bowden (8)
Hursthead Junior School

WORLD WAR II

Sirens wailing,
Bang, bang! go the blazing firebombs.
As German bombers swoop through the air overhead,
Locals run out of their houses in haste as they wonder where
the house opposite is.
There is a layer of rubble covering the cobbled street,
Cars and shelters are spread over the whole road.
Firemen pour out of the remaining shelters attempting to put
out the house fires.
The homeless watch in fear as these mighty fires increase at the
blink of an eye.
Fear is shown in the animals as you see the reflection of the fire
in their eyes.
Troops patrol up and down the road as the timing of their
march is perfect.
Night-time comes round - the blackout is commencing.
Blackout wardens inspect every house, occupants are questioned if a
glimmer of light seeps through their blinds.
Posters are spread on every wall possible advising on what to do and
what not to do.
Residents of the street cannot get an ounce of sleep, they dread the start
of another anxious day.

Adam Crowder (10)
Hursthead Junior School

FEARS

My fear is the darkness
For it is very scary
It's like a big black blanket
Covering us all

The moon is the curve of a cat's claws
And the brightness of the sun
My fear is the darkness
For it is very scary

The stars are sprinkles of glitter
Floating in the sky
My fear is the darkness
For it is very scary

The shadows on my bed
Are just me and Ted
My fear is the darkness
For it is very scary

The noise from downstairs
Gives me the scares
My fear is the darkness
For it is very scary

The footsteps coming closer
Is just my mum
Coming to kiss me goodnight
My fear is the darkness
For it is very scary.

Emily Grencis (8)
Hursthead Junior School

CATS

Lean cats
Mean cats
Very, very clean cats

Inside cats
Outside cats
Stray cats
And scavengers

Fluffy cats
Or short haired
Happy cats
Or grumpy

Some cats are wild
Some cats are domestic
Some cats are timid
And some are tame

Some cats are extremely clever
And some cats are as light as a feather

Fat cats
Slim cats
Black cats
Or white

Lean cats
Mean cats
Very, very clean cats.

Olivia McGahey (10)
Hursthead Junior School

CRAZY, MAD

Dad
He's football crazy, he's football mad
Everybody wants him to be their football dad
No one ever calls him dumb cos I do that alone
Everybody gets in moods when Daddy's on the phone

Leo
He's skating crazy, he's skating mad
He's my brother, Leo and he's a skating lad
He's *very* annoying as everybody knows
He goes along on skateboards with his talents that he shows!

Mum
She's cooking crazy, she's cooking mad
She's the bestest mum that anybody's had
She is so busy with five children that she's got
She hasn't got the time which makes her lose the plot

Kris
He's tennis crazy, he's tennis mad
My eldest brother, Kris competes with Dad
He treats the house like it's his own
And all he does is moan, moan, moan

Ash
He's fitness crazy, he's fitness mad
He goes to the gym scantily clad
He plays lots and lots of sports
He's hardly got time to change his shorts

Jack
He's rugby crazy, he's rugby mad
He's my twin brother, Jack and he's a rugby lad
He goes and plays at Manchester as everybody says
He always wins the match, however well he plays

Now that is my poem of my family
And, oh yeah, I am Megan your host, your poet, that's me!

Megan Worne (10)
Hursthead Junior School

THUNDERSTORM

James came out of school one day in a thunderstorm,
He got struck by lightning and started to change form.

He turned into a rhino and then into a snake,
Through a puddle he slithered and cried, 'Oh, for Heaven's sake.'

The storm was getting worse, it turned into a blizzard,
Then before he knew it, he'd turned into a lizard.

He got up to the road he lived on,
Then he turned into a gibbon.

He jumped onto the nearest branch and swung from tree to tree,
Then in mid-swing he sprouted wings and turned into a bee.

He buzzed from bush to bush,
By now he was late and had to rush.

Just as he got to his door,
The sun came out and he was James once more.

His mother took one look at him
In her usual accent asked, 'Where've you been?'

James Manton (10)
Hursthead Junior School

THE MONKEY

He is always just sitting there,
He does not have a clue,
He does not think it rude to stare,
The monkey in the tree.
He may live here in the jungle,
He eats a lot of food,
But he loves to play and bungle,
The monkey in the tree.

There he is, high up in the air,
Swinging on all the vines,
He does not even have to share,
The monkey in the tree.
His new life is so boring,
But he can be such fun,
Along the tree he is gnawing,
The monkey in the tree.

Here he is now, all so happy,
He's laughing all the while,
He's playing with his friend, Hatty,
The monkey in the tree.
Soon it will be time for his bed,
I can see he is tired,
Now it's time to rest his head,
The monkey in the tree.

Oliver Bristow (11)
Hursthead Junior School

CITY

The city is full of lots of things,
Houses and flats,
Skyscrapers and churches,
The park's full of birds,

Trees and a lot of flowers,
Lots of winding roads,
Full of cars and lorries,
The city, what a wonderful place.

Matthew Wells (11)
Hursthead Junior School

ME

I love playing around
In my garden, on the ground
My favourite colour is blue
And I'm a size one in my shoe

I like going to school
I like swimming in the pool
Because swimming is cool
I love animals, especially dogs
But I don't really like big, muddy hogs
I enjoy my life
And I am not a wife

I have a pet cat
Who loves lying on mats
He's always chasing lots of rats

I am shy
But I don't lie
I sometimes get in the way
But I didn't want to say

So that's my poem
Next time you need one
Just call me
Because I am always free.

Alice Semple (8)
Hursthead Junior School

FULL OF THINGS

That garden is full of wonderful things,
Like cats with whiskers, birds with wings,
The old trees creak with the strain,
The squirrels bury nuts and grain,
The lawnmower jolts as it cuts the overgrown lawn,
The old shed door gives a tired yawn,
The ginger cat spies the young mouse,
But quickly it sees her and scurries into the battered old house,
The blackbirds sing a joyful song,
The rabbit merrily hops along,
The mole that lives underground,
Snuggles against the slipper he found,
The ball that was thrown near and far,
Was next to the door that had been left ajar,
As night-time came the silence grew
And back down his hole went the little brown shrew,
Yes, that garden is full of wonderful things,
Like cats with whiskers, birds with wings.

Grace Hetherington (11)
Hursthead Junior School

PETS

My hamster is called Spooky
And my cat is called Webster,
Spooky is black
And Webster is black, brown and grey.
Spooky is so cute and Webster is too,
Webster is so furry and Spooky is too,
They make a happy couple together,
They love me and I love them.

Christopher Browne (8)
Hursthead Junior School

I DON'T KNOW

I don't know whether to laugh or cry
I don't know whether to say goodbye
I don't know whether to be happy or sad
Maybe I'm just going mad

I don't know whether to eat or drink
I don't even know what to think
I don't know whether to sit or stand
Or just to fly to another land

I don't know whether to love or hate
I can't even remember the date
I don't know whether to walk or run
Or go out and have some fun

I don't know whether to smile or frown
Or should I just lie down

I don't know whether to read or write
I wish I could give someone a fright
I don't know whether to shout or weep
I think I should just go to sleep.

Nicola Macleod (10)
Hursthead Junior School

BOISTEROUS DOGS

He loves his old cage and he's always in a rage
He loves his walks but he never talks
He hates poodles but he loves noodles
He loves to swim in the bogs,
He hates hot dogs.

Jonathan Coates (9)
Hursthead Junior School

MY IDEAL WEEKEND

There are so very many things
I really like to do
When the weekend comes around –
I just have to tell you

There's swimming and there's badminton
And playing with a ball
But there's one thing that's a joy to do
Which really beats them all

I can't wait to do my homework
Oh, it's such a lot of fun
Writing all the sentences
And doing every sum

Hours and hours of sweat and tears
Aching hand and brain
Too much of this is not enough
The pleasure's in the pain

And when at last the work is done
At the end of a long hard day
I feel so disappointed
'Cause it's time to go and play

So three big cheers for homework
Hip, hip, hip hooray
And if you disagree with me
Go get a life, I say!

James Cresswell (10)
Hursthead Junior School

MY ROOM

My room is a unique creation
But it is in need of decoration
It is a messy place
And there is no space
It is a disaster
With no carpet and no paper

I have a big room
That is messy top to bottom
I have a tiny bed
And if I had my way, I would paint the walls red
My toys are spread far and wide
I even have a TV on the side

The closet door opens wide
And you see the mess which is stored inside
Jumpers, T-shirts, socks too
All in a pile or two
I am at the back of the house
But I am not as quiet as a mouse

Don't worry
I am having wooden flooring
Also a new door
I am having the walls painted red
At the side of my bed
I've had a light
Built in my closet
I am having my room decorated
Better than it was before.

Ryan Healy (10)
Hursthead Junior School

MY CAT, PEBBLES

I have a really cute cat
She's really large and quite fat
Pebbles is her given name
She's rather quiet and very tame

Pebbles' fur is smooth like silk
Her favourite drink is creamy milk
She loves to sleep all through the day
It's hard to get her to come and play

She lies around on the mat
Hoping for a little pat
Sometimes she comes upon your knee
Until it's time to have her tea

She likes to wander all around
But when she's tired, she lies on the ground
She miaows and miaows and is quite loud
But of her we are always very proud.

Katie Thompson (11)
Hursthead Junior School

FRIENDS

Friends don't lie to you,
Friends are kind to you.
If you help them they will help you,
You can play with friends,
Laugh with friends,
Make things with friends,
So is your friend a good friend?

Philip Hanson (7)
Hursthead Junior School

TIGER

I have a cat that I adore,
His name is Tiger and I love him so.
His stripy coat of ginger and cream,
Truly as soft as a silky dream.
He really has the loudest purr,
Especially when I stroke his fur.
His long pink claws are as sharp as nails,
Just right for playing 'chasing tails'.
He has big, green eyes and a cheeky grin,
He looks through the window and says, 'Let me in!'
He loves to sleep, he loves to play,
That's how he likes to spend his day.
He has many toys around the house,
But his favourite is a big, black mouse.
I think all cats are just divine,
But I'm really glad that Tiger's mine.

Rebecca Thomas (10)
Hursthead Junior School

FOOTBALL

I like to play football whenever I can,
Especially in net, where I jump up and out like a fan.
The team that I like is Man United,
Whenever they play, I get overexcited.
My favourite player is Barthez of course,
He runs and jumps just like a horse.
He leaps and dives very far,
He drives around in a real fast car.
So football for me
Is a big chunk of my life, just as you can see.

Nick Delap (10)
Hursthead Junior School

SKATER IN HEAVEN

You should see how it feels,
Gliding along on eight rubber wheels.
Roller skating is like a dream,
But my skates are the best I've ever seen.
They're red and black, with fur inside
And the nice firm wheels, which will make you glide.
You can go up ramps and do a trick,
But if someone falls over, don't take the mick.
You can zoom along, jump over a bar,
Or do a 360 over a car.
When you are racing along on your blades,
It feels like you're free
And that's the end of my little story.

Daniel Newman (10)
Hursthead Junior School

BABY MAYBE?

Mum, Mum, please have a baby!
Mum, Mum, do say maybe!
Mum, you wouldn't have to do a thing,
Just think of the joy a baby would bring.
I would feed it and change its nappy,
The baby would make me very happy,
When you say no, it makes me sad,
Please say yes, I'll work on Dad,
Mum, Mum please have a baby,
Mum, Mum, do say maybe!

Sophie Fletcher (11)
Hursthead Junior School

MY PET HAMSTER

He's clever beyond dumb,
Who's barely ever glum.
He's called Cuddles
And he knows when to make puddles.
He loves his food
And he's never in a mood.
He's orange and white
And he's always right.
He loves maths,
Especially graphs.
He's never wrong
And he has a bit of a pong.
Who is he?
My pet hamster.

David Coates (11)
Hursthead Junior School

WATERFALL

When I was just a little girl
someone told me about a
waterfall
and this is what they said,
'Waterfalls
come crashing down
the water bounds
off the rocks
it makes a splash
it makes a splosh
but you'd better watch out
or you might get wet.

Elizabeth Kelly (11)
Hursthead Junior School

ARE WE THERE YET?

Are we there yet?
It's been a very long time
And we haven't yet had sight of the sea
I've packed my bag with lots of things
But I'm bored of them already
I should of packed the blooming telly

Are we there yet?
On our way we travel
We've had to listen to Mum's music
Why not some of mine?
My stomach has started rumbling
And we've still not reached the sea!

Are we there yet?
I really need the loo!
Mum says we're really close
Oh no! A traffic queue
My brother's feeling awful
And I think I feel awful too

Now we're having a picnic
Mum said it would be fun
But Dad's just been stung by a bee
So it's back to the car for my brother and me
We'll never get there and see the sea
This has been the worst journey
Are we there yet?

Charles Hartle (11)
Hursthead Junior School

SEASONS

S mall plants growing up from the ground,
P retty flowers all around.
R ed, yellow and other colours too,
I ndigo, violet and even blue.
N early summer, when it's really hot,
G rowing in the garden are apricots!

S un is dancing in the sky,
U nder the tree goes a fly.
M agic flowers grow from the soil,
M ysterious sky now smooth as foil.
E very kid's having a water fight,
R ain is unseen and it's warm at night!

A ll the leaves turn golden and fall,
U pset, the birds quieten their call.
T he animals hide away with their snacks,
U ntil the spring they can relax.
M ornings are darker and days are colder,
N ights are earlier and colours are bolder!

W et and cold, wind in our hair,
I n the garden the trees look bare.
N o longer is the sun in the sky,
T he birds hide away and refuse to fly.
E very road is covered in ice,
R eally slippy and not very nice!

Francesca Miller (10)
Hursthead Junior School

A River's Course

Towering mountain, morning sun
The ice is melting, the waters run,
Trickling down through streams so small,
As they tumble over each waterfall.
More water joins this growing race,
Now flowing down at such a pace.

Raging rapids gushing down,
Through the city and into town.
The river then goes into a lake,
Carrying boats that people make.
Our raging river starts to slow
And by the mile it starts to grow.

Meandering, winding away it goes,
Through the meadow it gently flows.
The river passes by the bay,
'What a beautiful place,' the sightseers say.
The river's course is nearly run,
The sea is here in the setting sun.

Sam Roe (10)
Hursthead Junior School

My Pet Snake

My pet snake was rather long,
It was blue and red with a bright green tongue.
He would wibble and wobble all through the day,
But he may scare all the neighbours away.
I woke one day to an awful sight,
My pet snake was black and white!
I took him to the vet for a vital X-ray,
It turned out he'd eaten Mum's black hairspray.

Matthew Drury (10)
Hursthead Junior School

I Am Ill

Today I spent the day in bed,
I had a terrible pain in my head.
I really was not very well,
It was like a witch had cast her spell.
I couldn't sleep a wink last night,
I gave my mum an awful fright.
My brother, George was not sleeping,
Because of my coughing and my sneezing.
My doctor said I was quite ill,
So he gave me a coughing pill.
Suddenly I felt much better,
So I sent the doctor a thank you letter.
The coughing stopped at half-past three,
Tomorrow I think it's school for me.

William Haddington (10)
Hursthead Junior School

Holidays

Miles from the ground and excited
Long wait, big frenzy
Luggage everywhere in its hundreds
Planes taking off and everyone's amazed
Ears pop, very quiet
Smells of petrol, seats in rows
Noisy announcements and babies crying
Loading bags near the engines
Cramped people on the plane
Long journeys, very bored
Airport, hungry and restless.

Adam Ramsden-Smith (10)
Hursthead Junior School

THE BOUNCING BALL

Flying high, flying low, watch that spinning ball go.
Smashing the ball to the other side, saying, 'Oh yeah, the score is tied!'
Skidding here, skimming there, forwards, backwards, everywhere.
Watching the ball until it drops,
Bouncing, bouncing, off it goes.

Flying fast, flying slow, watch that spinning ball go.
Forehand, backhand, volley, lob,
Puffing up lots of dust,
Yellow sunrise down below,
Bouncing, bouncing, off it goes.

Flying here, flying there, watch that spinning ball go.
Whizz, twirl, swoosh, zoom,
Getting tired? Watch out for the net!
This is now the end of the match,
Bouncing, bouncing, off to bed.

Gemma Kiersey (10)
Hursthead Junior School

MY HOBBY

My hobby is football, a very sporty sport
You can jump, run and kick,
There are lots of things you can do in footie,
Like score a goal and get the glory.
Football, football is the best,
Better than all the rest.
Football is passing, talent and skill,
The crowd going wild,
The manager shouting and dribbling up
Past the defender to the net, *goal!*

Alex Fripp (11)
Hursthead Junior School

How To Make A Monster

Chop up some eyeballs, throw into a pan with red food colouring
And stir-fry for thirty minutes,
Twist some tentacles round and round, throw these in a bowl,
Spread over some frog skin and flatten it out
And pop it in the oven for one hour.
Make some fat, now get the frog skin and spread it on to the fat,
Bake it for ten minutes, shape it into an oval.
Get a pack of twisted arms, take two, cover the arms with frog skin.
Add some sharp bear claws,
Fetch some witches' knobbly knees and cover with frog skin.
Now get a smaller piece of fat and cover it with frog skin
And make it into a sphere.
Now get a human's mouth without the teeth,
Now get some sabretooth tiger teeth,
Kill a snake and throw in the bowl and cook for five minutes,
Take that and the twisted arms and put them in the pan
Cook for two hours and when it's done you'll find yourself in a
Monster's belly!

Michael Roe (7)
Hursthead Junior School

A Recipe For A Haunted Birthday Cake

Get a bowl,
Pour in a pint of vampires' blood.
Mix in some eggs and a packet of bats,
Add a ghost and a witch.
Then add chopped spiders' legs,
Put in the oven,
Put on the spooky icing,
Then eat your haunted birthday cake.

Hannah Rakestraw (7)
Hursthead Junior School

PEOPLE OF NONSENSE

There once was a man called Harrow
Who liked to sing with the sparrows
Once he ate a pie with chips and gravy
Then went to join the navy

There once was a man called Mike
Whose favourite sports brand was Nike
His favourite food was fish and chips
And he also enjoyed it with fresh tomato dips

There once was a woman called Fay
Who only sailed her boat in May
She crashed on a rock and lost her frock
And was washed up on San Francisco Bay

Now these three strange people belonged to a club
And this club just happened to own a pub
Each night they would have a drink or two
And each be sick in a different loo.

Jonathan Chappell (11)
Hursthead Junior School

THE NILE

T   he Nile is very near the Equator.
H   alfway to the sea, a tributary called the Blue Nile joins the Nile.
E   mbankments, canals, basins and barrages were built to
     control the river.

N   early 6700 km long.
I   t's the longest river in the world.
L   ying beyond the Nile is a desert called the Barren Desert.
E   gyptians thought that Egypt was unique because of the Nile.

Kate Earnshaw (11)
Hursthead Junior School

MY PET CAT

Pebbles is the name of my cat
She eats a lot, which makes her fat
She sleeps on top of the stairs all day
And stays there till we come and play

Pebbles comes in from the storm
She sits in her bed to get nice and warm
She met my rabbits, they were washing their fur
But all she did was sit and purr

At night, Pebbles comes onto my bed
She's hoping for a pat on the head
She likes to have her fur all clean
Everyone knows she isn't mean

When she's hungry and wants her tea
She comes along to find me
She has just started to miaow
So I will have to go . . . now.

Amie Thompson (11)
Hursthead Junior School

CATS

A cat is a fearless and wild creature,
It lies ominously in the grass waiting for its prey.
When it sees its prey go by, its day is fulfilled and then it acts dead sly.
It pounces vigorously with enthusiasm hoping its prey doesn't see it.
After it carries its prey to its master, dropping it to the ground,
It rubs its body affectionately in and out of its master's legs
                                        like a slalom.
Then it has a long snooze in its woven basket,
Dreaming of what it can mischievously do next.

Ben Devereux (11)
Hursthead Junior School

POLLY AND PERCY

Polly and Percy are black and white penguins,
With shiny wet skin and a bright-orange beak,
Feet that are webbed and look like ducks,
You surely can't beat their dashing looks.

They live in the Arctic with the cold and snow,
But fly away for their holiday in hot Mexico,
With beautiful flowers packed with bright colours,
For their holiday there's no better place to go.

Last Christmas Eve the penguins got married,
After they flew away to the freezing Antarctic,
Polly in her wedding dress glistening with pearls,
The snow came falling beautifully down.

For them it was a love-match in Heaven,
Until the iceberg they lived on split,
With the icy cold water and nothing around them,
They thought that divorce would be it.

Hours passed, days passed and soon a month too,
Nothing to see but the ocean so blue,
Lonelier and lonelier with pangs of hunger,
With not a soul to see but the whales in the water.

One day they saw on their cold frosty iceberg,
Yes can it be their true love once lost? Yes,
From that day onwards they stuck side by side,
And moved to Mexico to live an exciting life.

In their new home they lived for two years or more,
Playing happily in the golden white sand,
They lived to the age of ninety-eight
And had two children called Johnny and Kate.

Elizabeth Henshall (11)
Hursthead Junior School

THE COOKIE BOY

I used to love cookies,
I ate them all day,
Until I woke up one morning
And I looked a different way.

I looked in the bathroom mirror,
Talk about unlucky,
Last night I had turned
Into *a giant cookie!*

I went to school that day,
No one seemed to spot
My overnight transformation
To a chunky triple choc!

After school, I ran straight home
And jumped into my bed,
It was then I seemed to notice,
Crumbs crumble off my head.

I felt a sudden pain,
It gave me such a fright,
I felt down near my bottom,
The dog had took a bite!

After tea I went to sleep,
I didn't sleep very well,
But when I woke next morning,
It was the end of my living *hell!*

Matthew Oates (11)
Hursthead Junior School

MY HAMSTER

My hamster's name is Harry,
He's small and easy to carry,
I can put him in my pocket,
But my mum would make me stop it.

He has a bit of a passion,
For anything that's sweet,
Chocolate drops are all the fashion,
But carrots make him weep.

He's fat and round,
He never leaves the ground,
He has a hamster gym,
But never moves a limb.
Harry is my hamster and I love him very much.

Thomas Mortimer (10)
Hursthead Junior School

SUNDAY MORNINGS FOR UNDER 11S

Flying passes
Down the line
To the wing
Acceleration
To
Jet speed running
Then
A crunching tackle
Into the
Mud.

Patrick Bucknall (10)
Hursthead Junior School

BUBBLEGUM

I'm in trouble,
Made a bubble,
Peeled it off my nose.

Felt a rock,
Inside my sock,
Got gum between my toes.

Made another,
Told my brother,
We could blow a pair.

Give three cheers,
Now our ears
Are sticking to our hair.

Matthew Clarke (11)
Hursthead Junior School

MY GRANDAD

When he was younger
He was as fit as a fiddle
And nearly made it to the
Olympic games as a walker

He was there when I needed help,
As he grew old and frail,
I helped him through old age

I'm so sad he won't see me
Go to the Olympic games.

Colin Todd (11)
Hursthead Junior School

THE GINGER TABBY

The ginger tabby
is always happy.
He likes to sleep
in a big heap.
He likes to chase mice
and he likes to crunch at ice.
His hobby is climbing trees,
but he always falls on his knees.
He doesn't like hats
but he likes his favourite mat.
He fights all night
and will be sure to give you a fright.
He always brings in worms,
when will he learn?
His name is Tigger,
once he got stuck to a sticker.
He is my cat
and he is still not fat.
He is my ginger pussycat.

Katie Eddleston (11)
Hursthead Junior School

THE CAT THAT ADOPTED US

One day in May, a cat came to stay,
He didn't look like a stray
And he wanted to play.
He drank milk from a saucer and food from a dish,
His favourite meal seemed to be fish.
I made him a bed out of an old cardboard box,
But he preferred my drawer full of socks.

After two weeks he was well settled in,
So we began to think of a name to call him.
We thought about Tiger, we thought about Stripe,
But then we decided that Poshie was right.

Jack Green (10)
Hursthead Junior School

SWEET DREAMS

My room is neat and tidy,
Just perfect is what I mean,
I like it to be spotless,
Not dirty or unclean.

My bed is always made,
Shipshape is the theme,
If only this were true,
In fact it's just a dream.

Robert Blease (11)
Hursthead Junior School

MY BOOK REPORT

I told my teacher why
I didn't have my work
I said that aliens took it
And flew off in the sky

I've always wondered why
On their journey to the stars
Those aliens stole my book report
And took it back to Mars.

Katie Dawson (10)
Hursthead Junior School

THE WEATHER

Weather is funny,
It always seems to change,
From rain to shining sun.
Wind and snow,
They always come and go,
When you're playing happily in the snow,
The sun will come and melt it all away.

Weather is funny,
It always seems to change,
When you're out at the park,
The rain will come
And that's the end of that.
As soon as you get home,
You look out the window
And the sun shines once more.
You go back out
And it rains once again.

At Christmas it starts to snow,
You're having fun,
Until a gust of wind
Comes tumbling by.

Weather is funny,
It always seems to change.

Jade Galtrey-Smith (10)
Hursthead Junior School

A RECIPE FOR A FAIRY

You will need a packet of fairy wings,
One wand and a magnificent dress.
Shred some flowers for her hair,
Make sure her head looks beautiful,
Then you can start putting flowers on her dress.

Next put some pompoms and glitter on the shoes,
Put some pink fluff inside the shoes
So they will be nice and warm
And there is your fairy.

Lydia Ross (8)
Hursthead Junior School

HOLIDAY

People playing in the sea,
People making sandcastles,
Waves splashing on the sand,
Boats fishing for food to eat,
Surfboards going up and down,
People snorkelling underwater,
People swimming in the sea,
A jellyfish hunting in the water,
Waves splashing on the rocks,
Lots of starfish in the sea.

Nyall Bhatt (7)
Hursthead Junior School

MY PARTY RECIPE

Wash the children,
Roast the balloons,
Roll the cake,
Crunch the candles when they're out,
Grind the food in your mouth
And melt the party bags,
Decorate with toys,
Scoop up the bouncy castle,
Simmer the music,
Mix it up, you have a party.

Andrew Powell (7)
Hursthead Junior School

THE LETTER

A letter came this morning,
I didn't know what was inside,
A white envelope with red writing,
Which read: *37 Oak Drive.*

I found it on the doorstep
When I was off to school,
I didn't have time to read it,
Because if I was late, I'd be breaking a rule.

I thought about it today,
That red writing stayed in my mind,
So when I opened it that night
What would I find?

I thought about it when Mum picked me up,
When we sat in the car,
Where had it come from?
Had it come very far?

I thought about it when Mum turned on the radio,
Even through my favourite song,
But when we got home that evening,
I found that it had gone!

'Where's my letter?' I asked in horror,
'Did I win some money? Is a cheque coming my way?'
'Sorry, it's bad news I'm afraid,' said Mum,
'It was your dentist appointment and it's today!'

Chloe Dowdle (10)
Hursthead Junior School

I ONCE KNEW A BOY CALLED TIM

There was a little boy called Tim
And to say the least he was quite dim.
He could not do addition
As he wasn't a mathematician.
At Christmas he would say,
'Happy Birthday, hip hip hooray.'
He loved to watch TV
And all he had was chips for tea.
His parents used to say,
'You should read every day,'
But Timmy did not agree.
He just sat down and watched TV,
He never did his work,
All he used to do was smirk.
He was no good at art,
In plays he was never the leading part.
He didn't even have one friend,
As Timmy drove them round the bend.
Tim couldn't listen or read or write,
When you asked him for a sweet, he was always tight,
'No, get your own,'
Was what he used to moan.
In the playground the boys were full of glee
And there was young Timmy looking bored as can be.
When anyone asked him to join in their game,
Tim's answer would always be the same,
'*No!*'

Philip Kent (11)
Hursthead Junior School

I Am

My name is Emma,
But really I am . . .
A joyful wild cat bouncing in the summer sun setting,
A rally car rushing through the countryside,
T&T fizzing over with bubbling anger.

But really I can also be . . .
Curry, so mild to the taste,
An exclamation mark ready at the shout,
A piece of algae swimming around untouched in the coral sea.

But really I can also be . . .
A dark blue wave crashing around on rocks with ferocity,
A light bulb always ready to help,
A sofa looking snug and warm.

But really I can also be . . .
A mansion looking through corridors searching unknown rooms,
Legolas from Lord of the Rings, ready to kill and very alert.

Emma Potter (11)
Kingsley CP School

There Was A Young Boy Of New York

There was a young boy of New York,
Who ate the world's supply of pork.
He ate all the bones,
Then gave lots of groans.
That silly young boy of New York!

Hayley Wright (10)
Kingsley CP School

A DART

A board pricker
A number picker

A fast flyer
A fun buyer

A point keeper
A big leaper

A fancy looker
A cork hooker

A catalogue to make me
A dart!

Lucy Philpot (10)
Kingsley CP School

I AM

My name is Edward Cox, but really I'm . . .

A hovering hawk tracking its prey,
A lazy bed sitting there all day,
A sleek racing car speeding down the track.

I'm also . . .

Ray Mears exploring the jungle,
A strong catapult that can throw really far,
A sturdy seaweed holding against the current.

But really I'm . . .

A helpful wire helping people make circuits,
A curious question mark always asking questions,
A fizzy cup of Fanta fizzing with energy all day.

Edward Cox (11)
Kingsley CP School

I AM AN ORANGE JUICE, BITTER AND SWEET

My name is Anna Feldman, but really I'm . . .

A badger hiding safely in its set,
A white van trundling along the road,
An orange juice, bitter and sweet.

But really I'm . . .

A long carrot, tall and straight,
A question mark, not sure what to do,
A prickly bush with a spiky temper.

I'm also . . .

A colour - violet with swirling moods,
A light bulb coming out with ideas,
A tall stool tucked away in a corner.

I'm sometimes . . .

A nodding dog without a nod,
A grand tower reaching up to the sky,
An information book, with writing jumping out of the pages.

I can be sometimes thought as . . .

A reader of lots of books, Garnet from Double Act,
A sharp-minded pencil writing reams.

Anna Feldman (11)
Kingsley CP School

I AM...

My name is Cassie Hesketh, but really I'm . . .

A hyena, laughing out loud,
A mini, dashing through the street,
Lemonade, bubbling as long as I can.

But I'm really . . .

A peach, short and chubby,
An exclamation mark, glowing on the page,
A sweet-smelling rose, with scent that fills the air.

But I'm also . . .

A smiley yellow, beaming all the time,
A phone, talking all day long,
A soft, comfy, bouncing bed.

But really I'm . . .

A spinning top, whirling round and round,
A house, holding heavy bricks,
A joke book, saying stupid things.

But I'm also . . .

Lisa Simpson, playing an instrument,
A T-shirt, waiting to be worn,
A file holding information!

Cassie Hesketh (11)
Kingsley CP School

I Am A Well-Placed Exclamation Mark

My name is Hannah Francis,
But really I'm . . .

A lone wolf prowling through the night,
A majestic eagle soaring through the azure skies,
A single bold mosquito buzzing in rage.

No, I'm . . .
A thrilling mystery story to read all night long,
A cold, black night, chilly but not without moonlight,
A raging, flickering fire frolicking amongst the trees.

No, really I'm . . .
A tall tree standing alone, towering above the rest,
An eerie graveyard, chilly and suspicious,
A well-placed exclamation mark jumping from the page.

No really, really I'm . . .
A spicy vindaloo, too hot to think of eating,
A slick sports car flashing my silver paint,
A cool, calm blue amongst other vivid colours.

Hannah Francis (11)
Kingsley CP School

There Was An Old Man From France

There was an old man from France,
Who decided to do a silly dance.
In the place he was dancing,
A woman was prancing,
That crazy old man from France.

Joshua Roberts (10)
Kingsley CP School

THE SKY

A cloud bearer
A rainbow wearer

A blue sitter
A sly spitter

A thunder creator
A weather curator

A sun supporter
A maker of water

A catalogue
To make me
The sky.

Esme Curtis (10)
Kingsley CP School

A SNAKE

A side slitherer
A venom giver

A silky rope
A scaled coat

A pattern hisser
A poisonous kisser

An angry creature
An evil feature

A catalogue to make me a
Snake.

Jessica Elliott (10)
Kingsley CP School

A Tiger

A stripe bearer
A zebra scarer

    A great biter
    A vicious fighter

A set of white paws
A set of huge jaws

    A tail wearer
    A moving shadow
    A pouncing predator

A catalogue to make me
A tiger.

Dyfed Thomas (11)
Kingsley CP School

A Book

A letter bringer
A song singer

A storyteller
A word cellar

A fantasy maker
A knee quaker

A film starter
A small darter

A catalogue
To make me
A book.

Sam Saunders (11)
Kingsley CP School

A FIELD

A seeder
A feeder

A picnic bearer
A cattle carer

A rain taker
A music maker

A wind shiverer
A hillside quiverer

A catalogue to make me a
Field!

Hannah Pomfret (11)
Kingsley CP School

A DOG

A claw like a dagger
A tail wagger

A fluffy hoover
A fast mover

A big creature
A small feature

A cat chaser
A bath hater

A catalogue to make me a dog.

Holly Byrne (11)
Kingsley CP School

A SNAIL

A slow mover,
A slime spreader,
A shell holder,
A creepy crawler,
A plant eater,
A silent mover

A catalogue
To make me
A snail.

Bryan Wright (11)
Kingsley CP School

THERE WAS AN OLD MAN FROM LEEDS

There was an old man from Leeds,
Who planted a packet of seeds.
One day he looked out
And gave a big shout,
For all he had planted was weeds!

Rebecca Capewell (10)
Kingsley CP School

THERE WAS AN OLD SAILOR FROM NEW YORK

There was an old sailor from New York,
But no one was interested in his talk.
He loved to play the fiddle
And to sit in the middle,
That friendly old sailor from New York.

Nicholas Chia (11)
Kingsley CP School

A MOUSE

A troublemaker
A cheese taker

A quick mover
A food hoover

A small nipper
A fast ripper

A catalogue to make me a
Mouse.

Abigail Moffat (10)
Kingsley CP School

THERE WAS A YOUNG WOMAN FROM SPAIN

There was a young woman from Spain,
Who was in a lot of pain.
To find her cure,
She must eat manure,
That smelly young woman from Spain.

Hannah Goff (10)
Kingsley CP School

THERE WAS A LITTLE BABY CALLED PETER

There was a little baby called Peter
Whose parents bought him a small heater
He was so very warm throughout the storm
That lucky little baby called Peter.

Erin Styles (11)
Kingsley CP School

I Am

My name is Emma Knowles, but really I'm . . .

A bear with a sore head,
Roaming around and growling all day;

A stretch limo, long and thin,
A white one, all fancy inside;

A cup of lemonade, yummy and sweet,
Always bubbly and bitter;

A scoop of ice cream, cold and cool,
A different flavour every day;

A question mark asking questions,
Roaming around, confused all day;

A blossom tree, happy in spring
But wicked in winter;

A bed, cosy and snugly,
Sleeping all day;

A teddy bear, soft and cuddly,
Nice and sweet;

A light colour, lilac, to make me happy,
So sweet and calm;

A fantasy talk with fairies, pixies
And elegant elves;

An understanding Arwen,
Elegant and calm;

A trainer, comfy and bouncy,
Bouncing here and there;

A pencil, tall and thin,
But likes to draw pictures.

Emma Knowles (11)
Kingsley CP School

A BEE

A pollen taker
A honey maker

A wing flapper
A flower trapper

A body of stripes
A load of swipes

A catalogue
To make me a bee.

Charlotte Connors (10)
Kingsley CP School

THERE WAS AN OLD LADY FROM LEEDS

There was an old lady from Leeds,
She collected lots of small weeds.
One gave a big shout,
So she threw the weed out,
That annoyed the old lady from Leeds.

Jonathan Storey (10)
Kingsley CP School

A PIG

A huge lump
A massive bump

A muddy puddle
A pink muddle

A curly tail
A giant male

A catalogue to make me a
Pig.

Sally Gleave (10)
Kingsley CP School

THERE WAS A YOUNG BOY CALLED TOM!

There was a young boy called Tom,
In his room he planted a bomb,
His room, it blew up,
The whole Earth, it shook,
That silly young boy called Tom.

Jack Perry (11)
Kingsley CP School

STAR

In the midnight sky, as black as tar
I saw a little star
All shimmering bright
It was making such a good light in the night
All dazzling, dazzling gold and bright!

Victoria Gilmore (8)
Kingsley St John's CE Primary School

BURNING EMBERS

Your blue and orange flames,
Dance around the black and smoky coke,
Turning it red and hot.
Keeping me warm, keeping me safe,
You are a giver of warmth and light,
On a cold and dark night.
Blazing away gloriously, so bright.
When you are hungry you will eat,
And change this energy into heat.
But will you ever fade away,
Or just die down and go away?
And will you ever come back to say,
How you brought light back to this dark day?

Victoria Lewis (11)
Kingsley St John's CE Primary School

MANY YEARS AGO

If I had been there in the times of darkness
When roaming kingdoms ruled the Earth
And castles were built to block out evil
With kings and princes being crowned
Great armies fought and lost their soldiers
Or lost an enemy as they'd lost theirs
But who was crowned the king of England
And who should lose against their foe?
When kings were crowned there would be a great battle
To choose the king to stop these times.

Francis Hunt (9)
Kingsley St John's CE Primary School

CUDDLY TOYS

I've got too many cuddly toys
Mum says they've got to go!
I'm hiding them all under my bed
Hoping Mum won't know.

They're my best friends, rabbit and duck,
They sleep with me in bed.
Mum's got the big black bin bag ready
The moment has come I dread!

I know that when I go to school
Mum will clear them out,
She'll pack them off to the jumble sale
Hoping I won't find out.

Sophie Reynolds (8)
Kingsley St John's CE Primary School

SNOWDROPS

Fluffy, white clouds covered the sky
A little bit of blue in the sky
White, fluffy shapes were falling from the sky
It covered the roads in bright white instead of black
I wonder what it is?
Of course, snow
Children ran out of the house
And dived in the snow
Making snowmen and snow-angels
After a while in the wind the children go home
And stand in front of a warm fire.

Stephanie Nicholls (9)
Kingsley St John's CE Primary School

THE BATTLE

It was a cold day
The trees jittering in the wind
When all at once the men charged
The ground vibrating like a drum

Swords clashed, arrows whistled
Through the air, plunging
Into the armour of the helpless men

Gallant knights fighting for victory
Blood lay over the battlefield
Death had taken over
Both sides gaining nothing until
One surrenders or flees.

Christopher Stubbs (10)
Kingsley St John's CE Primary School

THE SNOWBALL FIGHT

The snow landed thick and white,
A snowball went splat on the back of my head,
I picked up some snow and launched one back.

So soon everyone was throwing snowballs,
The bell went, everyone started groaning.

When we came back out,
The snow had melted,
We all felt rather sad.

Simon Stubbs (8)
Kingsley St John's CE Primary School

A Day In The Park

One day in the park
There was a dog with a great bark
On the other side there was a swing
Swaying like a wing
There was a little girl looking up
She said to her brother, 'Shut up!'
Her mother caught her
But she blamed it on her brother
But she didn't fall for that
And then came flying a bat
It even stole Dad's hat
There were loads of kids playing
Mother saying, 'We've got to go.'
But kids said, 'No, we're staying.'

Ben Stoddart (9)
Kingsley St John's CE Primary School

The Devil

The Devil is a scary thing
And if you see him, run away
For if you don't he will say,
'I am king of the underground
So come with me and we will rule the world.'
But if you do just one thing wrong
Then he will truly say,
'It's the end of your days my friend
And you can't run away.'

Harriet Waites (9)
Kingsley St John's CE Primary School

ALL SPORTS

A football match is good to play,
Because everyone cheers throughout the day.
A basketball game is good to cheer,
When you are winning all the year.
A netball match is good to play,
Because we practise through the day.
All these sports I like to play,
Because it keeps me fit each day.

Sophia Smith (8)
Kingsley St John's CE Primary School

COUGHING

Coughing, coughing all the time,
Cough in the bath, cough in the hall,
Coughing, coughing in a line.

Coughing, coughing all the time,
I really just want it to go away.
Whatever I do, it just wants to stay!

Catriona Gilmore (8)
Kingsley St John's CE Primary School

WHEN IT SNOWS

When it snows, I always goes
Deep in the forest where nobody knows
So fluffy and white, the snow falls down
So shimmering when it hits the ground
But when it melts, you always think
Come back next year, please, please, please.

Catherine Hunt (7)
Kingsley St John's CE Primary School

WHEN I SEE A RAINBOW

When I see a rainbow, my heart fills with love,
For others I care for, that's what I feel when I see a rainbow!

When I see a rainbow, I smell happiness and hope,
And I feel there's a chance, that's what I smell when I see a rainbow!

When I see a rainbow, I can hear the angels sing,
Their tunes fill my imagination, that's what I hear when
I see a rainbow!

When I see a rainbow, my eyes see peace, not war,
I look at no starvation and poverty, that's what I see when
I see a rainbow!

When I see a rainbow, I seek a land of peace, love and hope,
A place far from my reach, that's what I wish for when
I see a rainbow!

Jemma A Grayburn (11)
Mossley CE (VC) Primary School

THE DAY I WAS ILL

I thought I was brill
Then I got ill . . .
I was off school for three months
I think I ate too much lunch.

When I went back to school
I wasn't cool!
No friends
To last to the end.
I wish, I wish, friends could last to the end!
Next time, I'll go to school
No matter what!

Sally Bursnoll (11)
Mossley CE (VC) Primary School

BEST FRIENDS

It doesn't matter if you're big or small
Cos my best friends have it all.
I couldn't ask for better ones
My best friends are journeys to the sun.

My best friends are just the same
All they have are different names,
They wrap up warm every day
You should hear the things they can say!

We are best friends, which is great,
I couldn't ask for better mates.
They are the bestest friends I could ever have,
But I don't like it when they're sad.

We are best friends which will never change,
We are happy through sun and rain.

Kirsty Loach (11)
Mossley CE (VC) Primary School

WINTER'S DAY

Icy snow falling from the sky,
Hitting the ground, so soft and kind,
To walk along it you and I
While the turkey roasts.

Sitting by the fire, nice and warm,
Waiting for the people who live next door.
Getting the party ready, just us two
Come on be quick, 'cause we're waiting for you.

Kathryn Player (10)
Mossley CE (VC) Primary School

THE MOON

Alone in the sky at night
The moon shines silvery bright,
Surrounded by stars
And planets like Mars
It is quite a beautiful sight.

The moon looks like a lantern
Always on full beam,
It seems as though it's always there
With a brightly glowing gleam.

The craters are like little hills
Bumpy paths with tiny frills,
Winding round on their way
Round and round every day.

The moon always has a smile
Shining over every mile,
We look up to the sky and see
It's watching over you and me
Like a brightly glowing tile.

Lauren Wilson (10)
Mossley CE (VC) Primary School

WHEN I GROW UP

When I grow up I want to be
someone who swims in the sea
or I could be . . .
A teacher in Year 3

When I grow up I want to be
someone who could fell a tree
or I could be . . .
A leader in philosophy

When I grow up I want to be
good at maths like an actuary
or I could be . . .
Someone that's just like *me!*

Rachael Hutchison (11)
Mossley CE (VC) Primary School

TIME

I wonder what the time was
When time began?
I know what the time is now
But I don't know what it was then!

Time is a funny thing,
Yet it helps us every day.
We can be early or late,
But it will lead us in the right way.

I wonder what time looks like,
Is it fat and small?
Does it look like me,
Or is it thin and tall?

I wonder what the time will be
When the time ends?
7.00 or 8.00,
9.00 or 10.00?

I wonder how time works,
I really wonder how?
But I know this for sure
I'm happy with the time right now!

Catherine Cox (10)
Mossley CE (VC) Primary School

IMAGINATION

Imagination is a wonderful thing,
I wonder where it all began
Was it found at the top of the tallest tree,
Or sizzled in a frying pan?
Without it I could never dream
Of flying or sailing the seas.
Do you think that it can be locked away?
Do you think there is a key?

Perhaps imagination lives
Somewhere up in the clouds,
With all its fellow friends like,
Friendships, cares and doubts.
Maybe it is an animal
And prowls along the grass,
With huge violent, slashing claws,
And piercing eyes like glass.

I think it is so many things,
Many more than I can say,
But I know one thing that's for sure,
I treasure it every day.
I gaze in wonder,
Daydream too,
Thinking about those things,
Things that I've always wanted to do.

Chloe Boyes (11)
Mossley CE (VC) Primary School

WHAT AM I?

I had two lives
I live underground now
I brought my possessions with me
I lie here covered in sand

I see Tutankhamun sitting in his silver chair
I am in pitch darkness
My home is the underworld
I am the Egyptian mummy.

Jade Tomlinson (9)
Murdishaw West Community Primary School

WHAT AM I?

I was found by Howard Carter
I was wrapped in line bandages.
My heart has been weighed
I have a coil on my head
I wear white clothes
I am sitting on the throne
A black wig adorns my head
I live in a burning desert
I lay in my coffin.
I am an Egyptian mummy.

Paige Mills (8)
Murdishaw West Community Primary School

THE MUMMY

I see Osiris sitting on his golden throne,
I hear bones snapping from the gnawing gnash
Of Ammut the terrible monster.
 I smell the sweet grape wine, drunk in my honour.
I touch the fur from the precious cat that I have for a pet.
I feel that I am alive in Egypt.
    Me, the mummy.

Liam Dougan (9)
Murdishaw West Community Primary School

WHO AM I?

I was all wrapped up
Howard Carter found my tomb
I am ruled by Osiris
My death mask lies in a museum
And I have a curse on my body
I lived in the Eighteenth Dynasty
I had two stillborn daughters
I was nine when I was crowned
I was eighteen when I perished.
    I am Tutankhamun.

Martin Mawdsley (9)
Murdishaw West Community Primary School

EGYPT

E   gyptians grew crops by the busy River Nile,
G   lazing sun blazing on Egypt.
Y   ellow fire crackling in torches,
P   apyrus reeds squashed to paper.
T   errifying murdering, cursed tombs.

Liam Jackson (8)
Murdishaw West Community Primary School

A SENSE POEM

I see the god Anubis waiting.
I hear the voice of Osiris shouting.
I smell dried up natron.
I touch my linen bandages
I feel at home.

Michael Whitehead (9)
Murdishaw West Community Primary School

WHAT AM I?

I was very rich
I liked music, like the flute
I had special people to do my work
And the special people built me temples
I have nothing left inside me
I live in a special life
I am an Egyptian mummy.

David McAdam (8)
Murdishaw West Community Primary School

EGYPT

E nchanted Egypt is a mysterious place
G littery and bright, the sun shines down
Y ears go by, but the pyramids still stand
P yramids stand there, lonely and bare
T he River Nile gives life.

                  Egypt.

Jessica Voss (8)
Murdishaw West Community Primary School

EGYPT

E gypt is a dangerous place with dangerous animals
G olden scarab beetles scurrying across the floor
Y ellow sand, just lying there, very still
P apyrus written by artful scribes.
T utankhamun buried in his tomb.

Josh Yates (8)
Murdishaw West Community Primary School

EGYPT

E   gyptian people grow food by the River Nile
G   olden hieroglyphs written by entertaining scribes
Y   ellow sand covers my body.
P   apyrus blows in the feverish desert breeze
T   utankhamun lies in his blue and gold death mask.

Egypt.

Amy Hogan (8)
Murdishaw West Community Primary School

EGYPT

E   gypt is a hot country
G   old sun, shining through the beautiful blue sky
Y   ellow sand lying still
P   apyrus reaching towards the golden sun
T   utankhamum, the very rich pharaoh.

Egypt

Sarah Fitzpatrick (8)
Murdishaw West Community Primary School

EGYPT

E   mbalming fluid was put on mummies
G   olden death masks shine
Y   ellow sun sets
P   apyrus was woven into boats
T   respassing in a pyramid.

Terry Gould (9)
Murdishaw West Community Primary School

ME

I see my heart being weighed by Anubis
I hear my blood draining from me,
I smell the waxy smell of resin.
I touch my valuable death mask,
I feel I have been forgotten,
Forever!
Me, the mummy.

Carla Ami Davies (8)
Murdishaw West Community Primary School

ME

I see the underworld now I am dead.
I hear the scarab beetles scurrying by.
I smell the desert and the muddy Nile.
I touch the coolness of my case.
I feel proud to be in the underworld with Osiris.

Jason Southern (8)
Murdishaw West Community Primary School

EGYPT

E   gypt is a place where great pyramids stand
G   olden sand lies both sides of the Nile
Y   ellow, sparkling sun, shines all day.
P   haroahs ruling the ancient land.
T   utankhamun lies in his coffin, all alone.

Emma Jane Parkinson (8)
Murdishaw West Community Primary School

EGYPT

E gypt is a very hot place
G littering sun shines up and down
Y ellow golden sand in Egypt
P aprus grows very tall near the River Nile
T he people serve Tutankhamun in Egypt

Egypt.

Sophie Kavanagh (8)
Murdishaw West Community Primary School

THE MUMMY

I see the darkness of my stone tomb
I hear the voices of muttering slaves
I smell burning fire torches
I touch my pale, constricting bandages
I feel terrified as the voices glide past my coffin.

Me, the mummy

Lewis Stevenson (8)
Murdishaw West Community Primary School

EGYPT

E gyptian hieroglyphs up on the walls
G olden sand lies across the desert.
Y ellow sun in the sky
P yramids are orange.
T utankhamun was a very rich man.

Chloe Green (8)
Murdishaw West Community Primary School

EGYPT

E gypt, the land of black mud
G host slaves still serve the Pharoah
Y early the Nile overflows
P apyrus made into paper
T he people in Egypt worshipped their gods.

Egypt.

Ashleigh Parry (9)
Murdishaw West Community Primary School

EGYPT

The land of Egypt is very bare,
Houses made from rich, black mud.
Ancient cats worshipped in the temples,
The Nile flooding every summer.
Crops growing by the bubbling water,
No freedom for the working slaves.

Christopher Dixon (8)
Murdishaw West Community Primary School

ME

I see the sunless underground
I hear bones twisting
I smell a mouldy smell
I touch the scarab beetles
I feel life flickering inside of me.
Me, the mummy.

Sam Walker (8)
Murdishaw West Community Primary School

EGYPT

E   gypt is one big mystery
G   iza is the pyramid in Egypt
Y   ellow sand lies on the desert floor
P   riests are printing on papyrus paper in the pyramids
T   ombs and temples are full of demotic hieroglyphs.

Callum Roberts (8)
Murdishaw West Community Primary School

MY SISTER'S BONKERS

My sister's bonkers
About all her conkers,
She's got one hundred and twenty
I think that's plenty.
But she still wanted more
So we looked on the floor,
There was nothing around
Only the ground.
So we went to see
If there were any up a tree.
There were only ten
But we couldn't reach them!
She was getting quite vexed
About what to do next.
Till along came a dadda
Carrying a ladder.
My sister shouted, 'Yes!'
And in a minute or less
She had her hands on the conkers
Which over, she was bonkers.

Laura Sleath (9)
Offley Junior School

THE SEASIDE

I want to go down to the sea today,
To watch the shimmering waves,
I want to go down to the sea.

I want to go down to the sea today,
To feel the tickling seaweed,
I want to go down to the sea.

I want to go down to the sea today,
To taste the salty water,
I want to go down to the sea.

I want to go down to the sea today,
To smell the fish and chips,
I want to go down to the sea.

I want to go down to the sea today,
To hear the band playing,
I want to go down to the sea.

Michaela Jenkins (10)
Offley Junior School

HOW WAR FEELS

When the war began
It was horrible,
Too horrible to be true.
It was so dark
You could not see a thing,
I was scared,
I saw bombs.
How would you feel?
Why did it happen to us?

Vanessa Coppenhall (8)
Offley Junior School

WASTE OF MONEY

Little Master Johnny has a thing for sweets,
He likes junk and chocs
Not veg and meat.

He went to the shop with a pound to spend
And bought some strawberry laces with fizzy ends.

Then he walked back home with the sweets in his pocket,
Chewed a chew, then sucked a Locket.

His tongue felt like it was about to *explode!*
As if the sweets had unlocked a self-destructing code.

He walked down the street but tripped on a stone,
The sweets were dirty so he left them alone.

He had gone to the shop with a pound to spend,
But it wasn't all worth it right at the end.

Ross Field (10)
Offley Junior School

WINTER

Snowflakes falling all around,
Make a frost-white carpet on the ground.
Tucked in bed, all snug and warm,
Jack Frost runs across the lawn.

Snowmen stand, freezing cold,
On the lawn all *big* and bold.
Big warm fires full of coal,
Hedgehogs hibernating down a hole.

Spring is coming and then summer,
Slowly getting much, much warmer.
No more cold until next year,
When the cycle starts again.

Natalie Williams (10)
Offley Junior School

I DON'T WANT THAT!

I don't want steak and greens,
I don't want designer jeans.
I want parties and fancy dress
I want Coke and piles of mess!

I don't want a mansion, big or small,
Not in a city with a mall.
I want to be in the desert, under a tent,
Better than a mansion . . . no rent!

I don't want a ginger cat,
I don't want the Cheshire plains - cold and flat,
I want a tiger, big and strong, for when it gets windier
We'll travel to the mountains of India.

I don't want a red, shiny van,
I don't want to be Zinedine Zidane.
I want a motorbike and drive to Peckham,
I want to bend it like David Beckham!

Of all the things that are not the best
I know I really would detest,
Cleaning and tidying my room,
I'd rather ride my scooter - *vroom!*

Oliver Farren (9)
Offley Junior School

NONSENSE, NONSENSE AND MORE NONSENSE

Every little person in every little house
Is never as quiet, quiet as a mouse,
But still all the adults do their boring stuff
Like dusting all the ornaments and sweeping with a brush.

But still the kids are moaning all day long
And all the adults are hoping they could just sing a song,
But then one day everything changed
It turned completely the opposite way.

The kids went to work to pay the bills
While the adults played and basically just chilled.
But when the kids came home, mess was seen
And only the kitchen was reasonably clean.

Sophie Phillips (8)
Offley Junior School

SOMETHING'S FISHY

Sharks, fish and other sea creatures too,
Watch out for the crocodile, he might eat you!
There are fishes of many colours
Fishes that are quite dull,
I name the pink ones Freddy.

The purple ones are always ready
When the crocodile strikes.
The purple fish will scream, *'Yikes!'*
And flee for his life.
If he bumps into the shark that'll be . . .
        The end of him!
And if I fall into the water, that'll be the end of me!

Katie Jackson (10)
Offley Junior School

I LOVE THE WAY THE . . .

I love the way the trees sway,
I love the way the traffic flows,
I love the way the birds sing,
And how the wind blows, it blows.

I love the way the animals play,
I love the way the sun shines,
I love the way the leaves flutter,
And how the clock chimes, it chimes.

I love the way the tiger purrs,
I love the way the traffic lights change,
I love the way the buildings tower,
And how the snakes hiss in their cage, in their cage.

William Bordill (9)
Offley Junior School

WHAT AM I?

I like to bounce really high
Like my brother who reached the sky
I am made out of only one thing
If you drop me hard, I will ping
People use me just to be thrown
That's the life at my lovely home
You can put me in your pocket
In my body I'm in a socket

Guessed yet?

I'm a rubber ball.

Abigail Jones (10)
Offley Junior School

SEASIDE

The seaside is packed,
Each summer we all come back
With buckets and spades,
We play all the summer holidays.

The sea feels all cold
And the waves are gushing,
People buying ice creams
And are having loads and loads of fun.

We collect shells in our buckets,
Hold the shells to our ears,
We lie listening to the sea,
Until it's time for tea.

Siân Morris (10)
Offley Junior School

FRIENDS

One friend is ginger,
One friend is brown,
One friend has red hair,
One friend's a dumb blonde.

One friend has freckles,
One friend has spots,
One friend's quite normal,
The other one has lost the plot.

My friends are the best
You can't beat them
Because they're better than all the rest.

Yasmin Tredell (10)
Offley Junior School

MONSTROUS ME

I'm a furry monster
My toes are 3 feet long,
I'm pink and green and yellow
I communicate by song.

My hair's like toothbrush bristles,
My song is loud and shrill,
If you ask me to sing louder
You can be certain that I will!

I'm not a scary monster
I'm only 2 feet tall,
Compared to other monsters -
I'm really rather small . . .

My mum says I look silly
And so I guess she's right.
I never shout, or scratch, or bite,
I never even fight!

Stephanie Farrar (9)
Offley Junior School

FUN IN THE SNOW

S nowy weather having fun,
N ow the winter has begun
O ur red faces, cold noses too,
W e wrap up warm just me and you.
B utton eyes and carrot nose,
A bobble hat and ice for toes,
L ook at all the fun we had
L iving in the snow is mad!

Michael Urquhart (10)
Offley Junior School

MY CAT, BALOU

He's big, he's black
And slender too
He likes nothing more
Than to sit with you.

He spends his days lying around,
But wakes so easily at every sound.

Summer is his favourite time
Endless days lying in the sunshine.

He has been with us for 11 years
He's part of our family too
His name's unique I'll tell you why
Cos he's our cat, Balou.

Becky Dimond (9)
Offley Junior School

SUPER MUM

My mum is kind,
My mum is helpful,
My mum is super duper.

My mum is tidy,
My mum is clean,
She even washes up.

My mum, she never rests,
My mum, she always works
And that is why she's:

Super Mum.

Chris Howells (10)
Offley Junior School

ROUGH SEAS

Storms breaking
Ships shaking
Waves pounding
Skies clouding.

> Cold rain pouring
> Big ships roaring
> Gushing black waves
> Scary dull caves.

Sun coming out
Waves are not about
Lying on the beach
Ripples at our feet.

Rebecca Hudson (10)
Offley Junior School

MY NEW HAT

My new hat is black and white
It shimmers in the bright sunlight
It's made of felt
And it has a belt
Right around the brim.
I wear it for my
Dancing class
We stand in line
And dance and dance
Until our poor feet hurt.

Eleanor Baker (8)
Offley Junior School

WHERE TO SIT

'Now it's time to put you children, who I dread,
Into your literacy places,' the teacher said,
'Tina, Sarah, Joe, Emma, George and Amy May,
You will all go in the best - Group A,
Lucy, Ben, Ron, Hally, Faryaal and Alex Flee,
I will put you in . . . Group B
And Sandy, Amanda and Daniel Tea,
I'll put you in . . . Group C.'

'Group A will sit on tables one and two,
Group B on table three and four - go on, shoo
And Group C will sit on . . . wait on a bit,
There is no place for *you* to sit!'

'Sitting on the ceiling, without a doubt,
Will make our head teacher shout,
In the store cupboard - no point going there
Because that, in fact, is the caretaker's dog's lair,
Going on the field is absolutely crazy,
Because there lives a mad cow called Daisy,
In the library maybe - no, it's out of the question,
The only place big enough is the restricted section.'

'Oh dear, I've been so long going round the bend,
That it's now time for school to end.
Now go away, before I throw you in the bin
And tomorrow, could you bring another table in?'

Rachel Price (11)
Offley Junior School

THE ONE-WAY STREET

I'm the coalman who comes with the coal for your fires.
I travel along the one-way street on one-way tyres.

Good morning, I'm the postman with one-way feet
And I walk one-way along the one-way street.

I'm the sunshine who shines in the sky so bright
I travel one-way from morning to night.

Natasha Jane Wheatley (9)
Offley Junior School

THE HIGHWAYMAN

He'd a baseball cap on his forehead, a collar at his chin,
A coat of tiger's skin and jeans of fading blue.
They fitted very well, his trainers torn and ripped.
He rode on his bicycle, his wheels very shiny,
His wheels as shiny as bright yellow stars.

Over the bumps he rode with a bumpety bump.
He threw a stone at the window
And who was singing there, but the landlord's pretty daughter,
Playing with her long hair.
The sky was like a bag of coal being tossed up and down.
He played a love song on his flute,
It was like hearts flying up to Bess,
She was singing softly with some birds.
Bess, the landlord's daughter, the landlord's red-lipped daughter.

Christopher Owen (10)
Parklands Community Primary School

THINGS I'VE BEEN DOING LATELY...

Things I've been doing lately . . .
Baking with my dad
Doing little work
Playing with my best friend Luke
Picking my nose
Keeping it in a jar, *ugh!*
Tormenting my mum, *oooh!*
Going to my nan's for tea
Lolling on my chair
Deciding what to eat first
Doodling on my book
Dreaming lots
Trying my best
Biting my lips
Going mad!

Grace Boote (8)
Parklands Community Primary School

THE HIGHWAYMAN

The wind was not even a breeze and it was a very sunny day.
It was the best day for going to the beach.
When the Highwayman came running, running, running,
The Highwayman came running up to the golden beach.

He'd a Nike cap on his head and a Liverpool T-shirt on his body,
A pair of socks warming his feet and cool sunglasses hiding his eyes
And he ran with a jewelled twinkle,
His pistol butts a twinkle
Under the sunny bright sky.

Craig Evans (10)
Parklands Community Primary School

THINGS I HAVE BEEN DOING LATELY . . .

Things I have been doing lately . . .
Practising my times tables
Swimming with the class
Gazing into mid-air
Chatting to my posters
Eating sprouts and puking
Being particularly disgusting
De-fleaing the cat
Watching the cat be sick on the chair
Staring at my teacher
Pretending to work but snoozing
Trying to get out of class early
Twiddling with my hair till it's knotted
Doodling my name a million times . . .

Loving it - loving it - loving it!

Teresa Dowling (9)
Parklands Community Primary School

THINGS I LIKE AND DON'T

I like flowers
I like diamonds
Floating ones, glittering ones
Glittering everywhere
I don't like spiders
Lizards and snakes, *urgh!*
Things that make you happy
Things that make you sad
I like you and you like me
And that is that.

Amy Brothwood (8)
Parklands Community Primary School

THINGS I HAVE BEEN DOING LATELY . . .

Things I have been doing lately . . .
Dreaming about nature
Watching TV on my own
Drawing on my brother's head
Chucking mud bombs at Graham
Swinging on my chair till I fall off
Learning about poetry
Being good in school
Looking for worms and ants
Scribbling on my work
Counting on my fingers
Saving my drink till last
Pretending to be a lorry driver . . .

Worrying about my nan.

Luke Hughes (9)
Parklands Community Primary School

ALICANTE

See people walking quick like sneaking thieves,
Hear the birds shrieking like frightened children,
See birds going past like very fast Olympic runners,
Hear dogs barking like howling children.

Hear people babbling on and on,
Taste the salty sea when it is crashing against the rocks,
See people walking in and out of the shops,
Touch the very rough sand when you sit on it,
Taste of the very nice food,
See the shells getting brought up onto the surface.

Kirsty Jones (11)
Parklands Community Primary School

THE HIGHWAYMAN

The wind was as gusty as a rough sea.
The sky was as black as a forest.
With the clouds moving quickly
Like a ghost floating through a haunted house.
Down below, the winding road snaked towards the lonely cottage
And the Highwayman came galloping, galloping, galloping.
The Highwayman came galloping up to the wood inn.
He wore a hat as black as coal
With a duffel coat as black as a forest.
His trousers were as fitted as a shoe
And his boots were up to his thigh.
His sword twinkled under the dark blue sky.

Daniel Verschueren (10)
Parklands Community Primary School

RHODES

Feel the heat, like you're in an oven,
Smell cuisine as nice as people's breath,
Hear splashes in little doses,
See the pencil people on the left,
Taste ice cream as cold as frostbite.

Feel the cat's fur,
Smell fumes as scooters *brrrrrr,*
Hear mosquitoes make their noise,
See nothing but boys,
Taste sea water as salty as fish.

Rachael Horton (11)
Parklands Community Primary School

SPRING

Daffodils swaying in the wind,
Roses blooming red as blood,
Buttercups yellow, bright and beautiful,
Bluebells like raindrops falling.

Butterflies fluttering colourfully round the trees,
Kites are blown around and around,
Children playing happily together.

The sun shines like golden locks,
Squirrels jump from tree to tree,
Sheep are eating freshly grown grass,
Rabbits are hopping through the park.

Rivers are flowing through the forests,
It makes you feel quite relaxed,
Spring has come at last.

See the trees waving their arms,
Listen to the river trickling,
Taste the pure water as it rains,
It's as if you're in a dream.

See the flowers all different colours,
Hear the birds tweeting,
Smell the strong flowers,
It's as if you're in a dream.

See the beautiful birds flying round the trees,
Hear the howling wind,
Taste the juicy leaves,
It's as if you're in a dream.

Samantha Pennington (11)
Parklands Community Primary School

THE GHOST TRAIN

The clock strikes midnight,
Like a blue aurora, the train glows,
It's a transport bullet darting around,
Emerging from a tunnel like a roaring beast,
Listen to its deafening howl,
Hooting like a wounded owl,
It doesn't seem to cease,
Suddenly the brakes scream,
The air shifts out of the way,
The train puts chills down spines,
Slowly, steadily, silently
It whistles all the way,
But there is a whisper
Gliding round the bend,
Where it came from, nobody knows,
The sun arises, the train goes,
Only psychics hear the screaming sound.

Laura Greatorex (10)
St James' CE Junior School, Chester

THE GHOST TRAIN

Wailing out of the mist, it comes,
Surrounded by a ghostly blue aurora.
In the signal box the ghost of old Tom stands,
Grasping the levers with a ghastly, wrinkled hand.
Silently, it rattles along the track,
As it re-enacts its tragic death.
Faster, faster it goes rattling along the rusty, worn tracks,
Speeding into the night, screeching into the fog.
Then silence comes, as the clock strikes twelve . . .

Richard Heath (11)
St James' CE Junior School, Chester

GHOST TRAIN

Every night a new train comes,
Each one more spooky that the last,
Their roars are more fierce than a lion,
They charge round corners,
Releasing clouds of smoke,
They create a colourful light blue aurora,
They screech like eagles,
They glide into the station,
They have no brakes,
The driver gets off,
It's always the same driver,
But never the same train,
He goes in for a coffee,
He walks straight through the wall,
When he returns the train at once begins,
Then they put on speed,
Once they reach the water tower,
They vanish, vanish, vanish.

Christopher Henshaw (10)
St James' CE Junior School, Chester

A SNAIL'S DAY

Hiding in the bushes,
Travelling in my shell,
Looking at the birds above,
They're looking back at me,
Swooping down at me,
I escaped into the bush,
I'm safe and sound yet again.

Tom McIntosh (11)
St James' CE Junior School, Chester

DEATH AND DECEIT

Over hills,
Under hills,
In cities.
Out above space,
Middled in the mind,
On top of the tongue.
Around life, it waits, *then pounces*
And feeds on the heart and soul.
Upon its victim it spreads devious lies,
Inside shadows, it hides . . . waiting . . . for the kill.
This evil power lies silent . . . in the air.
High, low, life cannot dwell near this.

Michael Edward Stringer (11)
St James' CE Junior School, Chester

BLUE

Slowly, silently, now the sky
Walks the heavens in her blue dye.
Here and there she peers and sees
Shining fruit upon shining trees.
One day to the other she catches the sun
To have some midnight fun!
All crouched up waiting for the morning
The little boy all curled up and snoring.
His babysitter goes scampering by
With a flash torch shining in his eye
And glittering fish in the shimmering stream
The fountain sprinkles in the water's gleam.

Rebecca Randles (8)
St James' CE Junior School, Chester

JANUARY

Can't go skateboarding
But can do snowboarding
Can't see flowers
But can see snow
Cold outside
But warm inside
Can't have cold drinks
But can have hot drinks
Can't go outside in shorts and T-shirts
But can go outside in hats and gloves
Can't swim outside
But can swim inside.

Yes, December's passed
And that's no lie!
No more festivities, no more mince pies.
The only thing that's really true
Is that I've definitely got the January blues!

Gemma Williams (10)
St James' CE Junior School, Chester

NIGHT AND DAY

Night and day start a fierce battle
But the sun submits.
Darkness pursues the light.
The moon claims victory and the stars cheer
And then all is silent,
Until light starts to fight.
Then the sun will win and all is right
And it will be the same, night after night.

Leigh Cowieson (10)
St James' CE Junior School, Chester

WINTER

In winter I feel good,
I feel good, I can have snowball fights,
I feel good, I can build a snowman,
I feel good, I can make patterns in the snow.

In winter I feel bad,
I feel bad, it's too dark to play out,
I feel bad, it's not summer,
I feel bad, I get really cold.

In winter I look forward,
I look forward to spring so I can play out,
I look forward to not being so cold,
I look forward to being able to play on the grass at school.

I feel bad when winter's gone,
I miss the weather and the winter fire,
Looking forwards and backwards,
Through the seasons.

Jonathon Fairclough (10)
St James' CE Junior School, Chester

FUNERAL

A bracelet of eyes
Raindrops fall from black shadows
It's so silent - so eerie
Something sinks into the ground
A box of sadness and love.

Sophie Randall (11)
St James' CE Junior School, Chester

CATHEDRAL MEMORIES

The cathedral, quiet and peaceful
Gigantic, towering and vast
The organist climbs the steps
The organ's echo lasts and lasts.

The stained glass windows, brilliant and bright
Looked beautiful and fine
Lit by the sun's gleaming light
Sparkling on St Werburgh's shrine.

As I look up at the detailed wall
I hear the choir sing and call
The choir sounds like a cheerful laughter
I think of tunes and patterns long after.

As I leave through the giant-size door
I think of the decorated ceiling and floor
Looking back I remember the sights and the sounds
And the thoughts and the feelings that I found.

Rowan Metcalfe (9)
St James' CE Junior School, Chester

THE FAIRGROUND

In the fairground people play
on the rides all day.
Over there the ghost train stands
along the track which never ends.

Above me the Ferris wheel turns
around it goes, my tummy churns.
On the dodgem cars I ride
people chasing me, quick hide.

At the entrance people pay
to have a fun-filled day.
Inside the fairground it's time for me to go
towards home, oh no!

Hannah Edwards (10)
St James' CE Junior School, Chester

THE CATHEDRAL TRIP

Walking through the cathedral doors
I stare at the stained glass windows,
The sun shines down to make them alive,
It kind of feels like Christmas.

We all got into groups
Half of us had a long tour
And all the rest did activities,
Rummaging on the floor.

We listened to the very loud organ
After the really long tour,
It sounded like a monster
Bursting through the door.

Both of the groups swapped over
So we all did different things,
My group did tapestry
And I heard the choir sing.

As we grabbed our coats
And ran into the line,
We started to walk back home,
With memories in our minds.

Madeleine Ellis (9)
St James' CE Junior School, Chester

A SMUGGLER'S SONG

If you wake at twilight, to the sound of drumming hooves
Don't go peeping out the window, for anything that moves.
Them that asks no questions aren't told a lie.
Look away my darling, while the black riders go by!

Six and sixty horsemen,
Charging through the park -
Whisky for the parson,
'Baccy for the clerk;

Diamonds for a daughter, danger for a spy
And look away my darling, while the black riders go by!

Tom Watt (11)
St James' CE Junior School, Chester

PARADISE

Vines strangling all the trees,
Paradise,
Beautiful birds, insects and bees,
Paradise.

The sun plays games, making strange shapes,
Paradise,
Swinging through the trees are the apes,
Paradise.

Blistering heat all around,
Paradise,
Under the trees dangerous animals are found,
Paradise, or maybe not.

Joy Roberts (10)
St James' CE Junior School, Chester

THE CATHEDRAL

I step into the cathedral as quiet as can be
All the ceiling decorations I can see
Organ's sound pops my ears like it bullies me
Listening to its sound amazes me.

Monks stage with food and drink
Head of choir reading Latin Bible written in black ink
Stained glass windows some coloured in pink.

I did illuminated letters and did mine as an 'M'
I coloured mine in with a gold gel pen
I sat in Saint Werburgh's shrine feeling like I'm in a den.

Thomas Cresswell (9)
St James' CE Junior School, Chester

TIGER

I have a tiger with a big fat head
he takes up all the room when we're in bed,
I do not mind if he smells a lot
cos my mum says my room's already a pit.

He eats in the kitchen, he eats in the hall
he comes first time whenever I call.
He swallowed my jumper, he swallowed my hat,
and yesterday morning he swallowed my cat.

Tiger loves me, Tiger loves my mother,
but Tiger said he'll eat my brother,
I said, 'No Tiger, it will be such a waste
cos you don't even know how my brother will taste!'

Jayde Rhodes (9)
St James' CE Junior School, Chester

MY KITTEN DUSTY

My kitten Dusty jumps around the house,
She has a little toy, a catnip mouse.
When she plays with it she pulls it apart,
Then she starts racing, like a speeding dart
And sits on your lap and starts purring like mad.
When she wakes up she looks really sad,
Poor Dusty.

Everyone says that my kitten is cute,
She is only as big as my dad's boot.
I hug my kitten every single day,
But sometimes when I try, she starts to play.
At times my mum says Dusty's a real pain,
It's amazing, she is scared of rain,
Poor Dusty.

Stephanie Bate (10)
St James' CE Junior School, Chester

MY GRANDAD AND HIS GARDEN

My grandad loved his garden and in it he'd stay for hours
Planting plants and sowing seeds hoping they would become flowers.

He tenderly watered them and in pots he would them sow
Then sit right back and gaze a while and watch them bud and grow

My grandad loved his garden
His tasks would never end; he used to tell me often
That a garden without flowers is like a life without friends.

Jessica McLeay (10)
St James' CE Junior School, Chester

GHOST TRAIN

A fierce screeching whistle in the distance,
The scarlet train races through the ghostly mist,
Suddenly the brakes scream.

Hear the screeching sound,
Like a ghostly picture,
It speeds through the distance.

In the night, quicker than a cheetah,
The sun rises through the ghostly tunnel,
A whisper through the fog.

Katie Houghton (10)
St James' CE Junior School, Chester

THE TOUCAN

T   he toucan he flew
O   n a branch,
U   nderneath him was Cetur the anteater.
C   etur had some nice ants to eat. But
A   ll the ants ran away. Leaving
N   one for the toucan.

Kyle Cowley (9)
St James' CE Junior School, Chester

DARKNESS

The dark soot clouds over the sky
As the sun sinks, the shadows overpower the light
He demands the streets to be as silent as a graveyard
He clouds over the sky like dark soot from chimneys.

Luke Jarvis (10)
St James' CE Junior School, Chester

GHOST TRAIN

The ghostly hoot of the galloping train,
It chugs and chugs and goes insane.
The spooky pictures that glare at you,
The murdering screams that give you the chills,
The uncomfortable feeling that you're being watched.
The dead body that makes you wish you weren't there!
It's as empty as the desert
But the ghosts will still be there
If you like it or not!

Zoe Ednay (10)
St James' CE Junior School, Chester

SUN

Do you dare look into my blinding face?
I'm a million times hotter than lava!
Sunglasses won't protect you from my glare
I'll scold your skin from miles away
My shimmering face will light up your life
I'll burn you, I'll hurt you!
Don't trust me, never trust the sun!

Leanne Hurley (11)
St James' CE Junior School, Chester

DARKNESS

The dark sooty clouds meander over the sky's body
As the sun sinks its fantastic light.
The darkness demands its space in the busy sky,
It closes the sun's curtains as night beckons.

Sidharth Upendram (10)
St James' CE Junior School, Chester

MY DOG DEXTER

My dog Dexter is very crazy
He also is very lazy,
My dog Dexter is very small
You can hardly see him at all.

My dog Dexter is very mad
He's sensible sometimes, just a tad,
Dexter jumps like a lively frog
That makes him a very weird dog.

My dog Dexter runs very fast
When I race him I always come last,
My dog Dexter loves his bones
When we don't give him one he always moans.

Katy Fabian (10)
St James' CE Junior School, Chester

DARKNESS

As the sleepy sun sets and the
Silver streaks in the moon shine
Through the stars.

As the awakened stars shine and
The moonlit sky shines upon the
Sun slowly going to sleep.

As the children go inside because
It's getting dark, they all watch
The stars twinkle.

April Parry (10)
St James' CE Junior School, Chester

I WISH I WAS . . .

I wish I was a footballer like Michael Owen but taller,
I wish I was a karate kid,
Chop a piece of wood is what I'd do.
I wish I was a fire-fighter
That is a little braver, a little brighter.
I wish I was like Tony Blair,
I ruled the country just as fair.
I hope one day that I will be
And all of this isn't fantasy.

Christian Stabell (10)
St James' CE Junior School, Chester

MY ANNOYING SISTER

My sister is really annoying.
She walks in my bedroom without knocking,
Always wears my clothes without asking,
She sounds like a grandfather clock tocking.
All my friends think she's cute,
But I think she's a newt.

Micheala Dilley (10)
St James' CE Junior School, Chester

THE CATHEDRAL

A doorway shadow fills the empty air
The world outside is black and bare.
A candle flame with light so bright
Soft footsteps tread slowly down the aisles
Like people treading in snow piles.

As quiet as a pebble in a stream
I wonder silently around the great extreme.
Stood pausing momentarily in awe
I turn and walk towards the main door.

Sam Beech (10)
St James' CE Junior School, Chester

THE BIG THING

I liked dressing up as monks and nuns
I drank juice and ate some buns.

I heard the organ's very high notes
Then I had to get my coat.

The stained glass windows were wonderful
Now everything was colourful.

The cathedral is a safe place
It is also a very peaceful place.

Jake Green (10)
St James' CE Junior School, Chester

THE BATS

T he bats can glide,
H iding away quietly.
E yes glowing red.

B ehind the green trees.
A ll around me, twisting.
T he bats squeaking,
S queaking.

Kyle Lonsdale (9)
St James' CE Junior School, Chester

THE CAT FAMILY

Jaguars prowl the jungle at night.
They jump at some people and give them a fright.

Cats can jump at birds and frogs
But can also be scared of dogs.

Cheetahs run as fast as sound
They quickly get ready to jump and pound.

Lions have a furious roar
They also have great big paws.

Emma Dadson (9)
St James' CE Junior School, Chester

LOVE

Love is the colour of yellow, like the bright sun.
It smells like a fresh daisy.
It tastes like newly picked strawberries.
It sounds like the sea clashing against the rocks.
It feels like a soft dolphin.
Love lives in the sun.

Jade Jones (10)
St James' CE Junior School, Chester

AUTUMN APPROACHES

Autumn approaches
When the month goes away.
Leaves on the ground
Changing very slowly
When lying on the ground.

As autumn passes slowly by
The leaves' green coat
Turns to different colours,
As autumn flies by.

Kyle Cowley (9)
St James' CE Junior School, Chester

PURPLE LEAVES

Purple leaves,
Twisting,
Turning,
Floating.
Big,
Small,
Soft,
Multicoloured,
Breaking,
Leaves floating to the ground.

James Ison (9)
St James' CE Junior School, Chester

THE SUN

I have the ability to blind
If you look straight into my face
I will effortlessly burn you
If you are not careful
There are obstacles that stop
My fingers reaching you.

Mary Cooke-Fox (11)
St James' CE Junior School, Chester

A COLD, FROSTY MORNING

On a cold, frosty morning
I peer out of my window
and look around

I see the grass shimmer in the sun
I hear the leaves crunching under
someone's feet

I go downstairs and out through the door
people walk past me wrapped up warm
I walk past houses that smell like red apples

As I walk to school I see spiderwebs
glittering in the sun
they won't be there when I go home.

Samantha Proudlove (11)
St John's CE Primary School, Sandbach Heath

WIND

Creeping so slowly
Acting so lowly
Whistling a sorry song
Walking through the leaves
Weaving through the trees
Breathing through hair

Clothed only by a white mist
Veiled with a white gown
Gently touch anything she passes
Softly stepping
Gently walking
Hovering lightly.

Jonathan Lee (10)
St John's CE Primary School, Sandbach Heath

NOW YOU SEE ME, NOW YOU DON'T

I am a chameleon
Now you see me, now you don't
Changing colour as I move along
Now you see me, now you don't

I can blend into anything
Now you see me, now you don't
My range of colours doesn't run short
Now you see me, now you don't

I am a chameleon
Now you see me, now you don't
Changing colour as I move along
Now you see me, now you don't.

Naomi Bacon (11)
St John's CE Primary School, Sandbach Heath

THE DEATH RIDDLE

I rise from thy dead,
Of humans' death bed,
I rise with the souls,
Through the silent night, cold,
Through the silent farms,
To his ladies' arms,
You cannot see me,
You cannot feel me,
I am dead!
I haunt you!
I am not a soul or ghost,
What am I?

Michael Wellings (11)
St John's CE Primary School, Sandbach Heath

BIRDS IN THE SKY

Birds can swoop, birds can sing,
in the morning when it's spring.
They build their nests high in trees
and fly upon the warm spring breeze.
Their nests are made from moss and straw,
twigs and cotton plus much more.
Once complete they lay their eggs,
brown or blue ones, some with specks.
To feed their young they search for worms,
look in their beaks to see them squirm.
The fledglings grow, they try to fly,
just like their parents, high in the sky.
And once fully grown they leave their nest,
leave their parents and try their best . . .
To find a mate, to settle down,
To prove to their mummy they are fully grown.

Lucy Smith (8)
St John's CE Primary School, Sandbach Heath

THE SUN

The sun is a planet which is big and round,
Looking at it is out of bounds.
The sun is so hot,
It feels like a bowl of soup in a pot.
It looks like a bowl
Of something so foul.
The sun brightens the dark
To hear the dog bark.
The sun will go down the drain
Right into your brain.

Adam Coyne (10)
St John's CE Primary School, Sandbach Heath

THE WIND FROM THE WEST

A howling wind tapping at your windows,
When it's cold and frosty,
Whistling and wailing like a newborn baby,
Looks like a face in the heavy mist,
As it whispers in my ear I feel as if someone's
talking to me,
The wind carries the leaves.
It looks like a face screaming and crying
for desperate help.
It touches my forehead and its soft hand
moves gently across my cheek.
I feel like running, but I'm glued to the spot.
I know that it will be over in a matter of seconds,
But I stand there watching, waiting.

Sophie Desmond (11)
St John's CE Primary School, Sandbach Heath

THE WIND

In the dead of night
The wind is weeping,
For the soul of his is gone
With one last cry of sorrow,
His life seems to be fading,
It seems too hard to try,
He marks his love within his heart,
Morning's here at last,
The wind dies slowly,
The sun rises tearfully
And in her arms the soul lies.

Gabriella Silvester (10)
St John's CE Primary School, Sandbach Heath

FOOTBALL

F   ootball is a good sport.
    It is played all around the world.
O   ut come the players
    On the football pitch.
O   ff goes the whistle
    As the referee blows.
T   he footballers start to run around
    Passing, dribbling and shooting.
B   rilliant shots and saves are being made.
A   ll the players walk off the pitch for half-time.
L   ater the players keep playing
    It's nearly the end of the match
    It's still even.
L   ast minute in the match
    It is even
    The referee is ready to blow his whistle.

Max Davenport (11)
St John's CE Primary School, Sandbach Heath

HIM!

In the dead of night
He comes!
No one can see him
He goes to the house -
She hears a creak
He's there.
She looks around
An arm at her throat
A knife comes too
A piercing scream
Silence has come!

Anna White (11)
St John's CE Primary School, Sandbach Heath

PEACE

Peace is a light, fluffy-peach colour,
It smells of flowers and trees,
It tastes of light, creamy-white chocolate
           and vanilla fudge,
It sounds like sweet music,
Peace feels like soft sand slipping through
           your fingers,
It lies in our hearts.

Lauren Thornborrow (10)
St John's CE Primary School, Sandbach Heath

JEALOUSY

Jealousy is dark green.
It smells like boiling hot fire.
Jealousy tastes of gallons of vinegar.
It sounds like glass breaking.
It feels prickly and hard.
Jealousy lives in a lonely, dark cave.

Emily Geer (9)
St John's CE Primary School, Sandbach Heath

SADNESS

Sadness is grey,
It smells like bitter, salty water,
Sadness tastes like burnt cheese on toast,
It sounds like clean, rippling water,
It feels like tiny grains of sand,
Sadness lives in people's graves.

Jessica Lee (9)
St John's CE Primary School, Sandbach Heath

OLD AGE

Old age is the colour grey.
It smells like a cold winter's night
And tastes like dry dust.
It sounds like quiet whispering.
Old age feels like you are gradually falling asleep.
It lives in cold mountains.

Fiona Taft (9)
St John's CE Primary School, Sandbach Heath

WIND

The wind can be mild, the wind can be tough,
The wind can be a breeze on the early dawn,
The wind can be a very big, mighty storm,
Wind can be soft like a feather on your face,
The wind can be sharp like needles on your back
and then slowly fades away.

Rachael Willis (10)
St John's CE Primary School, Sandbach Heath

LOVE

Love is blue
It smells like yummy bread
Love tastes like cooked, smoky meat
It sounds like an enormous aeroplane shooting by
It feels like a little kitten rubbing around you
Love lives in the blue sky.

Jason Williams (9)
St John's CE Primary School, Sandbach Heath

GRANNY

My granny is not normal,
She has breakfast in bed at the table.
She loves going out, but always stays in,
Her dog is wonderful so she says,
Although it is a cat.
She always dresses in black
Because her husband is alive,
Funnily enough she never was married.
She lives in a bungalow and sleeps upstairs.
Granny has the heating on while it is the summer
And enjoys a lovely day at the beach while it is mid winter.
Some nights Granny has a quiet day in
Then ends up at the pub.

Claire Hellingman (10)
Shocklach Primary School

MONSTER UNDER THE BED

I've never looked under the bed.
Just as well, I think there's a monster under there.
Wait a minute.
Over there I saw six red eyes staring at me.
Something's coming out.
It has seven noses.
Eight arms.
And nine legs.
I think I should check it out.
No.
Better wait till I tell Mum.

Oliver Delf-Rowlandson (9)
Shocklach Primary School

MY BEST FRIENDS

My cat is like a jar of marmalade.
She catches mouse after mouse,
Which is fine when they're left in the stable,
But not when they're brought in the house!

My dog is as black as the fire grate,
He likes to lie at my feet,
But rattle his chain and he'll go insane,
For walking's his very best treat.

My pony is bay with a white stripe.
We love to hack round the lanes.
His favourite job is to gallop, jump and turn
At the slightest touch of the reins!

My animals are all my very best friends,
Each in their own special way.
They make me laugh, they make me smile,
I love them more each day.

Rebecca Thomas (10)
Shocklach Primary School

DOGS

Neither scales nor stripes have I
but I sniff, sniff, sniff.
Neither horns nor hooves have I
but I run, run, run.
Neither wings nor antlers have I
but I bark, bark, bark.
Neither beaks nor webbed feet have I
but I have a very cute face.

Charlotte Jenkins (9)
Shocklach Primary School

MY NANNA

It's raining, it's pouring
My nanna is snoring
I want her to play
But she's far away
I went to Ted
He nodded his head
I went to ask Peter
He was fixing the heater
I went to Mark
He said it was going dark
I went to my dad
He told me he was sad
I went to get a Coke
I heard my Nanna - she's awoke!

Ryan Michael Jones (8)
Shocklach Primary School

PLAY TIME

On the computer all day,
What do the teachers say?
They stand there and shout,
'Out! Out! Out!'
Some children hide,
Some go outside.
When the teachers go away,
The children come out and play.
When the bell rings, *ring, ring, ring,*
The children come in to sing,
While all is still on the computer.

William Davies (10)
Shocklach Primary School

MY BEDROOM

I want a snooker table in my bedroom,
But Mum says that I can't have one.
I don't see why not really,
Cos I could move my bed around
And there would be loads of space for it.

I would like to buy one with my money,
But Mum says that is not a good idea.
I don't see why not really,
Cos it would be better than CDs
And we could have loads of fun on it.

If I keep nagging, she may give in,
But my mum says that 'no' is the answer.
I don't see why really,
Cos it is my bedroom after all
And I should be able to have it there.

I would like to trampoline on our beds,
But my mum says they are to sleep in.
I don't see why really,
Cos they are nice and bouncy
And we do only sleep in them at night.

When I grow up, I will do all these things,
But my mum says she doubts I will.
I don't see why really,
Cos I will be able to do as I like
And it will be in my own house, not hers.

Fraser Clark (10)
Shocklach Primary School

WHO AM I?

Neither hoof nor trotter have I,
But I roam the jungle
And I'm free, free, free.

Neither spots nor wrinkled skin have I,
But I pounce on predators
And I'm free, free, free.

Neither hair nor feathers have I,
But I have fur
And I'm free, free, free.
    Have you guessed yet?
        I'm a tiger.

Emma Ewins (10)
Shocklach Primary School

MY PONY PING

My pony Ping
Is always up to something.
He rolls in the mud,
He eats too much grub.

My pony Ping
Is a funny old thing.
He always laughs
When he sends me flying,
But I wouldn't be without
My pony Ping.

Sam Westrip (8)
Shocklach Primary School

THE BLOODHOUND

I am the dog world's best detective,
My sleuthing noise is so effective.
I sniff the guilty at a distance
And then they lead a doomed existence.
My well known record for convictions
Has earned me lots of maledictions.
From those of trail of crime I scented
And sent to prison unlamented.
They either must avoid temptation
Or face my terrible accusation.

Daryl Baker (11)
Shocklach Primary School

MY HOBBY

Riding my pony is the best,
Galloping over lush green grass
With the wind in my hair,
Jumping every fence and hedge in sight,
Splashing through water then
Riding into the sunset to come home.

Helen Duley (10)
Shocklach Primary School

DOLPHIN

Neither hooves nor daggers have I, but fins
and I jump, jump, jump.

Neither tusks nor trunk have I, but rubbery skin
and I dive, dive, dive.

Neither wings nor feathers have I, but flippers
and I leap, leap, leap.

Neither spots nor stripes have I, but glowing eyes
and I play, play, play.

Aisling Cooter (9)
Shocklach Primary School

HOLIDAYS

H   ot days that are sunny
O   n the big balcony
L   ying in the sun
I   f of course the weather's hot
D   ancing all day
A   nd eating outside
Y   ou and me are playing together
S   o happy today.
     It's the holidays, hooray!

Tabitha Lord (8)
Shocklach Primary School

MY FAMILY AND ME

My family and me you must see,
Holly is my sister, she is so small
And not very tall at all.
Joshua is my brother, a footballer to be,
Maybe not, but we will see.
Lewis is the baby of us all,
All he does is just crawl.
As for me, I'm the coolest of them all.

Alice Charlton (8)
Shocklach Primary School

MY BEDROOM

My bedroom is pink and cream
And green and white.
It has soft, cuddly toys
But,
There is a gap,
A gap in the floor
And from the gap in the floor
Comes a light from the TV.
I like the cream and pink
And green and white,
But not that noisy crack of light.

Sarah Hellingman (8)
Shocklach Primary School

IT WAS SO QUIET THAT . . .

It was so quiet that I could hear
flowers sipping water
like dogs lapping water from their bowls.

It was so quiet that I could hear
electricity running through the wall
like the stream running through my garden.

It was so quiet that I could hear
pictures in a book screaming to get out
like prisoners in a tiny cell.

It was so quiet that I could hear
a banana trying to get out of its skin
like a butterfly trying to get out of its cocoon.

Alice Walton (10)
The Firs School

IT WAS SO QUIET . . .

It was so quiet that I could hear the moon
Coming up like sea gently whooshing on the sand.

It was so quiet that I could hear the sun
Laughing like a clown in a circus.

It was so quiet that I could hear vegetables
Growing underground like a plane soaring high into the sky.

It was so quiet that I could hear a battery
Creaking and straining to work like an old piece of wood about to
snap off a branch.

It was so quiet that I could hear a fly
Breathing like a powerful fan.

It was so quiet that I could hear the clouds
Chattering like a crowd of noisy people in a debate.

Kitty Green (9)
The Firs School

IT WAS SO QUIET

It was so quiet I could hear a blade of grass grow
like curtains rustling in the wind.

It was so quiet I could hear the clouds talking
like children chattering in a playground.

It was so quiet I could hear dust fall off a shelf
like an elephant walking on concrete.

It was so quiet I could hear skin form on custard
like the wind slowly blowing through trees.

Katie Greenwood (10)
The Firs School

SOUNDS OF A PARTY

Shouting and screaming
We're here, we're here
Get the football out
Bang, yeh
We won, you lost
5-3 to us
I'm starving
Lunch is ready
Crunch, crunch
Yum, yum
Singing merrily
Ring, ring
George, we're going
Come on
When everyone has gone
Rip, rip
I really wanted that
I had great fun
Goodnight Mum.

Roseanna Yeoward (10)
The Firs School

IT WAS SO QUIET . . .

It is so quiet in my room
I lie and listen in my bed,
The blankets murmur and I hear
The pages of the book I read,
They sigh and whisper in the dark.
I hear my slippers gently tread
And as I snuggle down to sleep,
My pillow breathes a slumber deep.

Camilla Bird (9)
The Firs School

WINTER TREES

By our house there is a forest,
With big, white, laden trees.
People come with their dogs,
Not knowing what is waiting for them around the bend,
Because I think they're spooky, scary, stark and spooky.

They look so still and silent,
As the only sound you can hear
Is the wind blowing around their branches.

I think they look mysterious,
As the branches look like claws
Waiting to grab you with their sharp tips.

Their branches are weak and their trunks are fat.
I think they're skeletons of the night.

Lucy Smalley (9)
The Firs School

IT WAS SO QUIET . . .

It was so quiet I could hear mould grow on the fruit,
like healing skin on a cut.

It was so quiet I could hear strands of hair
fall off my dog Alfie.

It was so quiet I could hear
church mice whispering.

It was so quiet I could hear the crowds roar
when Beckham scored a goal for England 40 miles from home.

Becky Okell (9)
The Firs School

PECULIAR PETS

Imagine some guinea pigs who ate pickled figs,
Imagine a pony whose TV was Sony,
Imagine some cats who loved taking SATs,
Imagine a dog stuck in a very soggy bog,
Imagine some pheasants who opened all my presents,
Imagine a mare who danced at a fair,
Imagine some kittens wearing pink and purple mittens,
Imagine 80 goats who drank 10 muddy moats,
Imagine some hens who wrote with quill pens,
Imagine a snake whose best friend was Drake.
    Imagine . . . imagine . . . imagine.

Catharine Verity (10)
The Firs School

THE AGEING HOUSE

Beneath my feet the floorboards creak
Beside me shutters bang in the wind
Around me there's no life apart from the life in me
In front of my eyes I see before me giant webs as well as the spiders.

Nathan Turnbull (11) & Dominic Percival (10)
Wincham CP School

THE AGEING HOUSE

In front of the house, an old rusty gate.
On top of the house, cracked tiles.
Down below in the cellar there are wine bottles
covered in cobwebs.
Around me are echoes from my footsteps.

Scott Liddle & Connor Mills (10)
Wincham CP School

TEACHER FOR SALE

Mrs Taylor-Carr, our class teacher,
Is up for sale quite cheap.
We tried locking her in the cupboard,
But the key we had to keep.
She writes on the whiteboard,
Gives lines out,
She needs better subjects
And tends to *shout!*
She's in the sale,
Just 50p,
If you come now,
Her desk comes free.
Geography or science,
Art or history,
How she knows it all,
Is a mystery!
She makes us do games,
Out in the cold,
So please contact us
And get her sold!

Olivia Gillespie (10) & Rebecca Paton (11)
Wincham CP School

THE AGEING HOUSE

Outside a rusty, old gate sways.
Beyond there is tall, swaying grass.
Through the door you will find a long, dark corridor.
Beneath the stairs there is a cellar with dusty, old wine bottles.
Above, the broken stairs hang on with their last thread.
Around the playroom a dusty horse rocks back and forth.

David Short (10)
Wincham CP School

CATS

Mouse-catchers
Feet-warmers
Top-runners
Great-hiders
Fish-spyers
Good-sleepers
Flea-homegivers
Tree-climbers
Prey-seekers
Body-rippers
Meat-eaters
Flesh-chewers
Soft-cuddlers
Garden-strollers
Territory-guarders
Body-cleaners
Plate-lickers
Top pets.

Bianca Huyton (10)
Wincham CP School

THE AGEING HOUSE

In front of the ageing door lies an overgrown garden
Behind the ageing door lies a labyrinth of passages
Underneath the creaking floorboards is the cellar
Inside the cellar were ghostly sights, dead bodies everywhere
On top of the bodies, the bats had nested their young
Above the bats the battered old spiders span their new webs
Will anyone live here again?

Thomas Speak (10)
Wincham CP School

FOOTBALL (NONSENSE VERSE)

We took kick-off at the end
The shot went over with a lot of bend
The referee took the keeper's kick
And it hit a player and made him sick.

The manager was playing striker
Because Van Nistlerooy became a biker
He shot the ball high on the ground
And then the linesman put in the rebound.

He headed it in like a headless clown
And scored to make them 1-0 down
The player was blasted into the goal
And then it all started when the whistle was blown.

Rhys Burton (10)
Wincham CP School

EATING THE GERBIL (NONSENSE VERSE)

Eating the gerbil, feeding the sweet,
Giving all the food each a little seat,
Making breakfast for the sun,
Getting up for tea at half-past one.

Eating the gerbil, walking on air,
Seeing a path which was very rare,
Morning stroll - I saw the moon,
Wondering what was a cartoon.

Eating the gerbil, drinking a tart,
Now I've finished, it's just the start!

Megan Rourke (9)
Wincham CP School

BROTHER FOR SALE

Podgy and fat,
Comes with a cat,
Seven years old,
Might have a cold,
Hair blond and short,
Also comes with a wart,
His name is Josh,
He's not very posh,
If you ring Jake now,
He comes with a cow,
He's only 50p,
The cat's called Lee!

Jake Smith & Michael Blythe (10)
Wincham CP School

THE AGEING HOUSE

Inside me are dusty cobwebs
Outside me are nettles and thistles
Down below in my cellar are dusty bottles and crumbly stairs
Up in the attic, cobwebs hang from the ceiling.

Oliver Pemble (10)
Wincham CP School

MY BOOK (NONSENSE VERSE)

I always read my book,
But I've not even started it.
I read it from the back to the front,
While standing as I sit.

It seems like common sense to me,
To read it while I play.
I've never even started it,
But I read it every day!

Rebekka Millington (10) & Carys Williams (11)
Wincham CP School

FISH

School swimmer
Danger watcher
Roof-like body
Crafty catcher
Baffling breather
Sleek shape
Bubble blower
Sound seeker
Finny friend.

Rachel Pogson (10)
Wincham CP School

RHINO (NONSENSE POEM)

Rhinos are green with pink spots,
Once I saw one down at the shops
With a black handbag,
It still had the price tag.
His name was Henrietta,
He'd gone to post his letter,
With the bill for the bag
Which still had the price tag.

Samantha Payne & Stephanie Berry (11)
Wincham CP School

THE AGEING HOUSE

Outside there is an old, messy, overgrown garden,
Down below my feet there are brown, crisp autumn leaves,
High above my head there is a clear blue sky,
In the middle of two tall oak trees is a battered bench,
Around the edge of the garden there are pretty roses,
In the centre of the garden there is a broken, dusty statue.

Sophie Snelson (10) & Mel Hughes (11)
Wincham CP School

LIMERICK

There was an old lady from York
Whose favourite food was pork
Whether cold or hot
She didn't care what
That greedy old lady from York.

Cara Evans (10)
Wincham CP School

LIMERICK

On a cold, sunny Monday last spring
Britain had appointed a new king
His name was King Louis
His nose was all gooey
That cold, sunny Monday last spring.

Michael Evans (10)
Wincham CP School

THE MAN LAST SPRING (NONSENSE VERSE)

When the leaves fell down last spring,
I heard a bit of a ping.
A man went pop
And he could not stop,
He landed on a car
And bounced into a bar.

Tom Baker (9)
Wincham CP School

LIMERICK

On a cold, sunny Monday last spring
I ran fast and heard something ring
I looked in my pocket
And found a small locket
It fell on the floor and went *ding*.

Adam Nield (9)
Wincham CP School

LIMERICK

On a cold, sunny Monday last spring,
The old church bells started to ring.
There were beautiful dresses,
Confetti made messes
And the choir started to sing.

Sophie Massey (10)
Wincham CP School

THE SICK OLD LADY FROM YORK

There was an old lady from York
Who really wanted to eat some pork
She ate two earwigs
Instead of her pig
That very sick old lady from York.

Cameron Fairweather (10)
Wincham CP School

LIMERICK

There was an old lady from York
Who sucked on some very red chalk
She got very dusty
And smelt very musty
That dusty old lady from York.

Benjamin James (10)
Wincham CP School

THE OLD LADY OF YORK

There was an old lady of York
Who ate 200 pounds of pork
She ate a piece of steak
And a bit of cake
That fat old lady from York.

Sam Apperley (10)
Wincham CP School

LOST: ONE PET

Oh, my loving pet,
He escaped from the vet.
He is a bit shiny
And a wee bit tiny,
Oh, please find my loving pet.

Nic Clawson (11)
Wincham CP School

THE PARK

Where the grass is damp and green,
Where the shallow streams are flowing,
Leaves danced on the ripples.
I ran to the water,
Sparkling like diamonds in the sun.
Slippery moss covered the rocks,
Making them look like velvet pillows.
Trickling water off the trees,
Spattered on the streams,
Where the sound of twigs snapping,
When the tiny mice came out at night,
Was the first chime of dusk.
The bats scattered off into the silent trees
And the beautiful smell of lilies, roses
And other ravishing flowers at the park,
Floated in the warm night air.
And the scrumptious taste of the
Blueberries, raspberries,
And other fruit at the pondside,
Tingled in my mouth.

Carey Griffiths (9)
Winnington Park Primary School

MY FIRST TRIP TO ANFIELD

The day had arrived,
The weather was great,
My first trip to Anfield,
I just couldn't wait.

At around two thirty,
We arrived at the ground,
The crowd were chanting,
A deafening sound.

The teams they did enter,
The battle began,
Opposing were Leeds,
Can we win? Course we can!

A pie at half-time,
Just what was needed,
The score was 4-0,
My team had succeeded.

Tom Mills (10)
Winnington Park Primary School

STORYTIME

S   ometimes during storytime,
T   om tiddles with his tie,
O   lly fiddles with his laces,
R   on roots in his lunch box,
Y   es, that's what most people do,
T   immy twiddles with his toy,
I   sabel sucks her hair,
M   e, what do I do best?
E   at an apple left over from my snack.

Tom Fishwick (8)
Winnington Park Primary School

SATISFYING SEASONS

Much pleasantness arrives with spring,
Firstly you can hear the birds sing,
Also the brightness from the sun,
Adds to everybody's fun.

Everyone loves sizzling summer,
It appears to make other things look glummer,
The water is ice when you go to swim
And wherever you look nothing is dim.

As for autumn where there are no leaves,
The world around grieves,
The skies are so dull,
To block its cold you get covered in wool.

The winds whirl in winter,
The dullness is one big splinter,
What never stops is the rain
And you're stuck inside; you'll go insane.

Then the cycle starts again,
The sun and the rain,
The winds howling
And beautiful blossoms prowling.

Jack Slater (10)
Winnington Park Primary School

CATS

C ute cats can feel the spirits in the night-blue sky
A nd furry cats can feel the spring
T imid cats are too scared to come out
S ome like you and some like us.

Aysha Barrett (8)
Winnington Park Primary School

STORYTIME

S ometimes we have storytime.
T oday we're having storytime.
O ur story is called 'Olive And The Dog'.
R obyn is exceptionally interested in this story.
Y ou might like it too.
T ime to start reading the story.
I t is really exciting.
M e and my friends love this story.
E veryone sits on the carpet.

Robyn Conway (9)
Winnington Park Primary School

FRIENDS

F reddy, fantastically clever against almost anyone,
R achel, right and never wrong in every lesson,
I sabelle ignores whilst the teacher's talking,
E mily excitedly enjoys everyone playing,
N athan, a naughty monkey in the classroom,
D aniel discovers something new every day,
S arah, silent as an angel anywhere she goes.

Emma Brown (9)
Winnington Park Primary School

FAMILIES

Families are hard work
And always very noisy.
Mum never stops shouting,
Dad tells me off non-stop.

Young little sisters crying like the rain,
I hide in my room,
Lovely and quiet,
Safe from the ferocious family members.

Annabel Johnson (9)
Winnington Park Primary School

WHAT DO YOU THINK OF ALL THAT?

My cat thinks he's a dog, sometimes he imitates a frog.
My cat thinks he's a dog, he even tried to pick up a log.
My cat thinks he's a dog, he even drinks from the bog.
My cat thinks he's a dog, he follows me for a jog.

My rabbit thinks he's a cat, he once chased a rat.
My rabbit thinks he's a cat, he is rather fat.
My rabbit thinks he's a cat, what do you think of all that?

Becky Healey (8)
Winnington Park Primary School

WINTER

W onderful whirling snowflakes white as snow.
I gloos are cold and icy winds blow.
N eat flowers in rows are sleeping till spring arrives.
T rees look like they are going to slide past the horizon.
E ven birds feel bad.
R ainy days make me feel sad.

Lauren Edwards (8)
Winnington Park Primary School

AUTUMN

A ll the orangey tanned leaves twirling to the ground,
U nusual behaviour as hibernating befalls the land,
T rees drop their leaves to sleep, like a child turning out the light,
U nder a blanket of coldness the land waits to be free,
M oths and other creatures plan their winter as hibernation falls,
N ow all is quiet except for the twinkling of the snow as it lies
                                        frozen over everything.

Omar Smith (8)
Winnington Park Primary School

THE FIRST STAR I SEE

The first star was like a crystal glimmering in the moonlit sky.
It smiled back at me like a wide, shiny ruby opening,
Wide for the midnight sky.
The glimmering star shimmered away to the glassy moon
And stood softly, calmly and golden
For everyone else to see.

Hannah Gregory (8)
Winnington Park Primary School

ME

My mum's gone on strike,
I haven't a clue why
And my dad's gone for a hike,
My nan's out playing footy,
I know that for sure,
My sister's out shopping,
Now she's bought the whole store.

My brother's gone to jail,
For burning down a sale,
The thing is they are weird
And nobody can see,
But that's probably because
They are different to me.

Ashleigh Fullwood (9)
Winnington Park Primary School

SUMMER

S   andy way shelter over you because summer is lovely.
U   ntidy bedroom I'm not allowed out in the summer for a day.
M   um going up the stairs to put her summer shorts on.
M   um putting the deckchairs out for a fantastic summer picnic.
E   leven days of summer, I love it.
R   avishing sun, in the summer we play out.

Chloe Johnson (8)
Winnington Park Primary School

SPRING

S   parkling showers of rain make ripples in the pond.
P   recious bluebells shimmer like midnight stars.
R   avishing sunflowers, bright yellow like the sun itself.
I   think of children wearing shorts and T-shirts.
N   ana and Grandad with their deckchairs out.
G   randad with his garden crammed full of beautiful flowers.

Kirsty Hassall (8)
Winnington Park Primary School

SCHOOL'S OUT

S chool really stinks
C hocolate is banned
H arry's gone haywire
O utside the sand pit has no sand
O lly's made a new friend, her name is Magnificent Myer.
L ouise just lit a match.
'S he's set the school on fire.

O ut on the football pitch Mr Davies stands, he really thinks
this isn't very grand.
U p the playground we all go, skipping merrily even though . . .
T he school's aglow.

Tommy Bullen (7)
Winnington Park Primary School

DRAGONS

Dragons
Spitting fire
Popping lava
Dragons
Sleep in volcanoes
Dragons
Strike like a cobra at their prey
Hot dragons
Burning hot like the sun
Dragons are
Beautiful.

Daniel Hayes (9)
Winnington Park Primary School

AUNTY PENNY'S WEDDING

At Aunty Penny's wedding, there was an awful worry,
Just because the best man lost the rings in stress and hurry.
I couldn't understand why we had to have the steak,
It made half of the guests too full to enjoy the wedding cake.
When the wedding dress ripped, Aunty Penny screamed,
It made an awful noise and the priest was not too pleased.
Then, later in the day, there came the evening do,
There was some dreadful karaoke that we had to listen to.
As we set off for home, my Aunty Penny cried,
Which clearly goes to prove she's still a little girl inside.

Rachel Bousfield (8)
Winnington Park Primary School

ELEPHANT

Mice-fearer
Heavy-weighter
Peanut-muncher
Insect-cruncher
Water-blower.

Sher Tang (10)
Winnington Park Primary School

RIVER

The water is calm, peaceful, silent, flowing,
Suddenly it splashes into some rocks,
Spray flies into the air splashing me like rain,
Then it gently flows on into the sea.

Adam Woods (10)
Woodfield Primary School

RIVERS

I used to be beautiful.
I would run down streams and waterfalls,
I would go past children
Playing in the fields.

I would see horses drinking from me,
Also insects on the ground,
Until nasty people came
And put packets in me,
Also old gates and pieces of metal.

Afterwards, when they'd finished,
I looked at myself and thought, *what a mess,*
And now I am just a dump.
I remember the days when I was beautiful
And I would run down streams.

Chloe Hunt (11)
Woodfield Primary School

THE BEST RIVER INDEED

Splashing bubbles over rocks
It came rushing through with speed
It is the best river indeed.

It came flowing by the apple tree
Whirling its way through
It came towards me.

Calmly it swam by
Past the meadows where I lie
The river takes its time.

Jodie Ankers (10)
Woodfield Primary School

THE LIFE OF A RIVER

Dodging the rocks,
Starting up high,
The stream is lonely
Looking up at the sky.

Getting quicker, faster,
Causing a river,
The smell of the water
Is making me shiver.

It is bold and strong,
Running towards the big rock drop,
The river has fallen,
Causing a stop.

The river has ended
In an estuary,
It's not lonely anymore,
Now it's in the sea.

Jack Berry (11)
Woodfield Primary School

RIVERS

Rivers are as blue as the sky and as clear as the sea.
The river tries to push through the mud
And so it has to go into a curve,
Then it goes into the sea.
The river goes down the mountains
And then it goes into the valleys and hills
And then it drifts away into the salty sea.
The other rivers come from sleet or snow.

Lydia Atkin (10)
Woodfield Primary School

LIZARD

Dragging my scaly skin across the ragged floor,
My eyes glowing in the dark,
Racoons hunting for rubbish, some playing,
Then an owl swoops down.
The sound of a hawk,
It smelt odd, like oil
And then a poacher popped out shooting the owl.
I was deafened by the sound.
I bit the owl on the toe,
It squirmed and dropped me.
I expanded myself,
My loose, scaly skin turned into gliding wings
And I glided over the city,
Hitting the forest tree to tree.
I heard something moving in the bushes,
It sounded like a snake,
So I ran into a cave calling for help.
But I knew it was no good.
It came following me and bit me,
I started to get sleepy,
I knew it was poisonous.
I felt a pain on my stomach,
I saw blood everywhere where he was sucking me in,
I felt like spaghetti getting eaten, but worse.

Ryan Vickers (11)
Woodfield Primary School

POLLUTED RIVER

Water flowing calmly,
Just watching it was good,
But now people throw rubbish,
I don't think they should.

Trolleys, car tyres, cans and wrappers,
Please don't throw anymore,
It used to be so beautiful,
It should be against the law.

Jamie-Lea Chadwick (10)
Woodfield Primary School

MY JOURNEY TO THE SEA

In the mountains is where I start,
Smashing small pebbles as I dart,
I plunge, I gush, I rush and race,
As I'm running I pick up pace,
I bash into huge rock and stone,
I slow and then I start to moan,
As I get calm I see my end,
Then I will meet my other friend,
I get wider and start to fear,
The sea is very nearly here,
I am now at the sea at last,
My single life has now just passed.

Sarah Howard (10)
Woodfield Primary School

WAR

War is red.
It smells like rotten dead people.
It tastes like a man's heart.
It sounds like people dying.
It feels like getting stabbed in the heart.
War lives in *Hell!*

Oliver Peace (9)
Woodfield Primary School

WATER

The rain falls heavily onto the grass,
With a splish, splosh, drip, drop.
A river runs down a mountain gushing to and fro,
Through caves, mud and snow.
The sea laps softly on the edge of the beach,
It looks as colourful as a peach.
Tap water streams out of taps,
Into a bowl of Fairy Liquid on top of some old maps.
Canal water is alive and full of mucky things,
Such as carrier bags, wrappers and Coke can rings.
Stream water flows very slowly,
It makes a trickling sound as it goes,
Like tea out of a teapot being poured into a cup.
Puddles are formed by rain,
They liked to be played in by children with wellies.
A lake is huge and full of fish,
Who swim all day without a single care in their minds.
Water is an important life source for this world!

Samantha Ricketts (11)
Woodfield Primary School

FLOWING MEMORIES

Little fish swim up and down,
Left and right, round and round.
Boats will sail to and fro,
Some with passengers, some for show.
People hungry for some fish,
Perhaps they'll get a tasty dish.
All these wonderful things we adore,
Pollution and rubbish has made them no more.

Philip Cadman (10)
Woodfield Primary School

CHRISTMAS SURPRISE

It's time for Christmas and I'm excited.
What will my presents be?
I can't wait to see what's in that box.
Right now I can't wait!
We will find out tomorrow and it will be fun,
But I want to know right now.
My father says, 'You will have to wait,'
And soon I'll be irate.
I just want to know what's in that box
But I'll have to wait!
It's now Christmas, let's go downstairs.
I can't wait.
'Mum, Dad,' I shout.
They come down and give me the box.
Now I find out it is a *computer!*

Thomas Allen (10)
Woodfield Primary School

A JOURNEY OF A RIVER

The sound of water trickling down a stream,
Running towards the river,
Weaving its way through the rocks,
From the marshy ground.
Faster and faster over the fall,
Calming down slowly after.
Gorging its way through the hills,
Curving in meanders slowly.
Wider and wider the river it gets,
Slowly but surely nearing the sea.

Alex Davies (10)
Woodfield Primary School

THE SEA

The sea is like a fairground
Surfing on the waves
Try to stay on the banana boat
Have you fallen off yet?
The sea has many creatures
Some of which snap at your feet
The slippery seaweed
Have you slipped yet?
The sea can spit
The sea can roar
The sea is salty
Can you taste it yet?
The sea can be rough
The sea can be calm
I don't like the sea
Do you?

Lucy Hallmark (11)
Woodfield Primary School

THE DISAPPEARING WATERFALL

Calm it was at the top,
Making no sound, not moving, sitting still.
But as it came down,
Mad angry it was.
If anyone walked in front, it would sweep them away.
It came rushing down the mountain,
Banging, screaming at the top of its lungs
And then calm it went
Flowing into the valley
And then to the mouth of the sea.

Wakia Chowdhury (10)
Woodfield Primary School

FOOTBALL MATCH

The football match is starting,
We'd better get to our seats,
Time to get the burgers,
The hot dogs and the sweets.

The players get into position,
The kick-off whistle's blown
And even only one minute in,
A great match is shown.

A great match here at the Millennium Stadium,
Liverpool are 2-0 up,
There it is, the final whistle,
They've won the FA Cup.

Andrew Rowntree (11)
Woodfield Primary School

THE FLOOD

The river was calm and quiet,
But all of a sudden the rain came
And the river was quiet no more.
The river had burst its banks,
Water gushed through towns,
Buildings, streets and homes.
The flood lasted for days,
But finally met the falls and ended.
The river that had burst its banks
Was now quiet and gentle again.
Many people died that night
In the terrifying waters.
Even buildings were taken under
By the rampaging water.

Michael Bailiff (10)
Woodfield Primary School

RACING CAR

Racing car, racing car, going round the track,
Racing car, racing car, not stopping until its tyres are flat.
I go round the corner at 100mph,
With the force and the power,
I smack into the barrier.
Oh no!
What's to do?
My feet are all blue,
I overtook one, I overtook two
And then I smacked into you (barrier).
Up comes the ambulance out of the blue
And takes me to the hospital for an X-ray or two.
The hospital tells me I will be fine,
But I will have to stay there for a month or nine.

Nicholas Risi (11)
Woodfield Primary School

THE SEA AND BEACH

The sea is so cold,
The sea is so bold,
The waves bouncing up and down,
Jumping like a clown.
People go there for sun and joy,
If they get bored, they can play with a toy,
People usually go in for a swim,
Over in the distance they see a shark's fin.
They always buy ice cream for family and friends,
Everybody hates it when the day ends,
The sea is calm when everyone's gone,
Splishing and splashing another day passed on.

Chris Rowntree (11)
Woodfield Primary School

WATER

I like water,
I could sleep in it.
I think there's too much water.
I like swimming in it, it's fun.
Drip, drop, drip, drop,
Someone's left the water running.
I watch the water as it fills the bath,
Gush, gush, goes the water.
Water falls from the sky in little drops,
As though someone turned the waterworks on.
Sometimes it comes heaving down.
I like water, it's fun.
If I was allowed, I'd swim in water all day!

Holly Magee (10)
Woodfield Primary School

SPEEDWAY

A race on speedway, the danger zone for some,
But not for the good ones the race was starting.
There were always crashes on speedway,
That's why they call it the danger zone.
3, 2, 1, go! The race had started.
There was a crash on the first bend.
Oh no, people watching the burning car now,
This is a disaster. We had to quit the race.
The fireman came, he put the fire out,
But the man inside was dead.
Now this was a disaster.

Adam Hughes (11)
Woodfield Primary School

MONSTER ON MY BED

It comes in when you're asleep.
It knows when you're awake.
Do you think it's a monster?
It creeps under your bed.
It slithers up the wall.
It walks up your cover.
It goes on your cushion.
It's just like a monster.
I wake up. Oh, it's only my teddy!

Michael Thomas (11)
Woodfield Primary School

HAPPINESS

Happiness is bright pink,
It smells like new flowers just come,
It tastes like new bread just from the store,
It sounds like laughter in the park,
It feels like a smooth dog,
It lives in the heart of everyone.

Michelle Stockton (10)
Woodfield Primary School

RUSHING WATER

I kneel before the river,
The colours are greeny-blue,
In the coldness I shiver,
I see the ripples run through.

I smell the scent of trees above,
I hear the near rushing water,
I look up and see a white dove,
I see myself getting shorter.

Abigail Banks (10)
Woodfield Primary School

THE LONG AND WENDING RIVER

R   ushing down at a violent speed
I   nterspersed rocks and weed
V   ultures high, the fish are low
E   nter the valley and start to go
R   iver gone, no longer there, meandering its way
                              without a care.

David Carter (11)
Woodfield Primary School

RIVER

I run calmly down the river bed.
I can feel the fish swimming through me.
I can see people throwing their junk in me.
I start to go faster and faster.
I am heading for a waterfall.
I gush down into rapids.
I go out into the sea.

Thomas Lewis (10)
Woodfield Primary School

LOVE

Love is red
It smells like red roses as they glisten in the sunshine
It tastes sweet
It sounds like a laughing, newborn baby
It feels like your head hitting the pillow
Love lives deep down in your heart.

Jade Hodgkinson (9)
Woodfield Primary School

HOPE

Hope is a shining yellow,
It smells like strawberries in summertime,
It tastes like fruit and sweets,
It sounds like a choir singing,
It feels like a big teddy bear,
It lives in the middle of the world.

Yasmine Harrison (10)
Woodfield Primary School

DESERTED RIVER

The gushing and pushing river
Came bashing down the mountains
And darted its way down.
It slowly calmed down
As it got closer and closer
To the deserted sea.

Samantha Cobby (11)
Woodfield Primary School

HEAT

Heat is orange.
It smells like burning wood.
It tastes like a red-hot flame.
It sounds like a fire crackling.
It feels like a warm fire.
Heat lives in the sun.

Bethany Edwards (9)
Woodfield Primary School

DEATH

Death is black,
It smells like smoke,
It tastes like blood,
It sounds like doors banging,
It feels cold,
It lives in the graveyard.

Pedita Lowe (9)
Woodfield Primary School

GHOSTS

Ghosts are white
They smell like tar
They taste like death
They sound like a train breaking
They feel like slime
A ghost lives in my house.

Sam Fletcher (10)
Woodfield Primary School